WHERE IS IT?

THE SIMON & SCHUSTER
COLOR ILLUSTRATED QUESTION & ANSWER BOOK

WHERE IS IT?

Simon and Schuster Books for Young Readers
Published by Simon & Schuster Inc., New York

First American Edition, 1985
First published in 1984 by Kingfisher Books Limited
Elsley Court, 20-22 Great Titchfield Street
London W1P 7AD
Text Copyright © Grisewood and Dempsey Ltd. 1984
Illustrations Copyright © Grisewood and Dempsey Ltd./
Librarie Hachette/Arnoldo Mondadori Editore S.p.A./1984

Published by Simon and Schuster
Books for Young Readers,
A Division of Simon & Schuster Inc.
Simon & Schuster Building
1230 Avenue of the Americas
New York, New York 10020

10   9   8   7   6   5   4   3   2
10   9   8   7   6   5   4   3   2   1   (Pbk)

Simon and Schuster Books for Young Readers
and colophon are registered trademarks
of Simon & Schuster, Inc.
Also available in Julian Messner Library Edition

Library of Congress Cataloging-in-Publication Data

Question & answer encyclopedia—where is it?
   Where is it?
   (The Simon & Schuster color illustrated question
& answer book)
   British ed. published in 1984 under title:
Question & answer encyclopedia—where is it?
   Includes index.
   Summary: Answers such geographical questions as:
"Where is Timbuktu?" "Where do pandas live?"
"Where was Atlantis?" and "Where does mud boil?"
   1. Geography—Miscellanea—Juvenile literature.
2. Children's questions and answers. [1. Geography—
Miscellenea. 2. Questions and answers] I. Lambert,
David, 1932-   . II. Bampton, Bob, ill. III. Title.

IV. Series.
G133.Q44   1988   910   87-32220
ISBN 0-671-55341-0
ISBN 0-671-55342-9 (lib. ed.)
ISBN 0-671-68468-X (Pbk)

Printed in Spain by Artes Gráficas Toledo, S.A.
D.L.TO:264-1989

Authors
David Lambert
Mark Lambert
Brian Williams
Jill Wright

Artists
Bob Bampton/The Garden Studio
Norma Burgin/John Martin & Artists
Oliver Frey/Temple Art Agency
Bernard Robinson/Tudor Art Studios
Mike Roffe
Mike Saunders/Jillian Burgess
Trevor Scobie/John Martin & Artists
Tammy Wong/John Martin & Artists

CONTENTS

PLANTS AND ANIMALS

THE PAST

PEOPLE AND PLACES

TRANSPORTATION

INDEX

PLANET EARTH

▼ WHERE IS THE GREENWICH MERIDIAN?

A meridian is a line of longitude, an imaginary line on the earth's surface between the North and South Poles. The Greenwich Meridian is 0° of longitude. It passes through the Royal Observatory at Greenwich, in London, England.

In 1675 the Royal Observatory was founded on a hill above the king's palace at Greenwich. Last century, a new transit telescope was installed to determine time by measuring the passage of stars. The meridian on which the telescope was situated was fixed as 0°. In 1884 this meridian was accepted as the Prime Meridian. All other lines of longitude are measured east or west of Greenwich.

▼ WHERE CAN YOU SEE THE SUN AT MIDNIGHT?

Near the North and South Poles it never gets dark in the summertime. The sun can be seen all day and all night – unless it is cloudy.

As the diagram shows, the earth's axis is tilted. In June the North Pole is tilted toward the sun. As the earth rotates on its axis, the entire area within the Arctic Circle remains in sunlight. So even at midnight the sun can be seen above the horizon.

In December, the South Pole is tilted toward the sun, and it is summer in Antarctica. The sun can be seen at midnight within the Antarctic Circle. But in December the sun never rises above the horizon within the Arctic Circle.

▼ WHERE IS THE MAGNETIC NORTH POLE?

A compass needle always points toward the magnetic North Pole. At present it is near Bathurst Island in northern Canada – over 930 miles from the geographic North Pole.

In 1831, James Clark Ross discovered the magnetic North Pole off the Boothia Peninsula in northern Canada.
   Today it is 496 miles north of this point. The location of the pole is mainly controlled by movements inside the earth which make our planet into a giant magnet. Over very long periods of time the earth's magnetic field can reverse, moving magnetic north to Antarctica. This has happened 30 times in the last five million years.

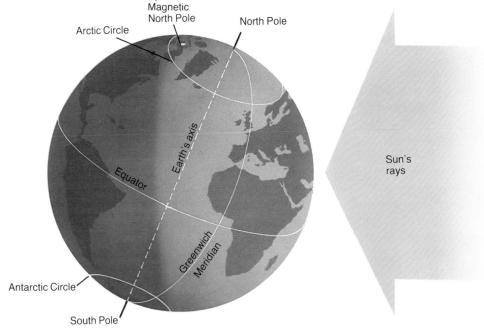

Magnetic North Pole

North Pole

Arctic Circle

Earth's axis

Equator

Sun's rays

Greenwich Meridian

Antarctic Circle

South Pole

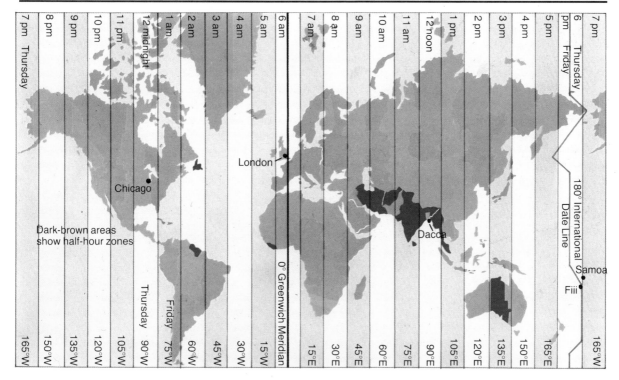

Top row (time zones, left to right): 7 pm Thursday | 8 pm | 9 pm | 10 pm | 11 pm | 12 midnight | 1 am | 2 am | 3 am | 4 am | 5 am | 6 am | 7 am | 8 am | 9 am | 10 am | 11 am | 12 noon | 1 pm | 2 pm | 3 pm | 4 pm | 5 pm | 6 pm Friday | 7 pm Thursday Friday

165°W | 150°W | 135°W | 120°W | 105°W | 90°W | 75°W | 60°W | 45°W | 30°W | 15°W | 0° Greenwich Meridian | 15°E | 30°E | 45°E | 60°E | 75°E | 90°E | 105°E | 120°E | 135°E | 150°E | 165°E | 165°W

Map labels: London, Chicago, Dacca, Samoa, Fiji, 180° International Date Line, Thursday, Friday

Dark-brown areas show half-hour zones

▲ WHERE COULD YOU HAVE A FOOT IN THURSDAY AND A FOOT IN FRIDAY?

The date changes at the International Date Line which follows approximately the 180° meridian. This meridian is on the opposite side of the world to the Greenwich Meridian.

The earth rotates on its axis through 360° in 24 hours. So there is one hour's time difference for every 15° of longitude. Since 1883 the world has been divided into the standard time zones shown on the map.

When the sun rises on a Friday at 6 a.m. in London (at 0°), it is already midday in Dacca (at 90°E) and it is 6 p.m. on Friday in Fiji (at 180°E). But westward from London, time is behind Greenwich mean time. So when it is 6 a.m. on Friday in London, it is midnight on Thursday in Chicago (90°W). In Samoa (170°W) it is 7 p.m. on Thursday. So when it is Friday evening on the Fijian side of the Date Line, it is Thursday evening on the Samoan side.

▶ WHERE IS THE HORIZON?

The horizon is the boundary where the sky seems to meet the ground or the sea. Because the earth's surface curves, things seem to disappear over the horizon.

The higher up you are, the farther you can see. On a clear day at the shore you can stand on the beach and watch a boat travel out of sight over the horizon. The curve of the earth prevents you from seeing it any more. If your eye level is 5 feet above sea level, the horizon you can see is 3 miles away.

If you climb to the top of a

98 feet | 49 feet | 5 feet | Sea level | 3 miles | 9.3 miles | 13 miles

cliff, you can see much farther, as the diagram shows. And if you climbed up a mountain to 9,842 feet above sea level, the horizon would be 124 miles away – if the weather was good enough to see that far.

▼ WHERE IS THE EARTH'S CRUST BEING FORMED?

New material is added to the earth's crust by volcanoes. Much of the lava is molten material from the part of the earth called the mantle which lies beneath the solid crust. Some volcanoes are found on land, but many are located deep beneath the oceans where lava flows onto the seabed.

Imagine an almost round egg with a shell that has been cracked in a number of places.

This is a good picture of our earth. The earth's outer layer, the crust, is somewhat similar to the eggshell. It is rigid; it is also very thin when compared to the diameter of the earth; and it is broken into a number of major and minor parts called crustal plates.

Some crustal plates, such as the Pacific Plate, are made entirely of ocean floor. Many crustal plates include whole continents as well as parts of the ocean floor. These gigantic plates are moving very slowly, and as they move, the continents move with them.

In some places the plates are gradually moving apart. As they do so, molten material from beneath the crust wells up and is added to the edges of each crustal plate. Such a boundary is known as a constructive plate margin, and the process of adding new material to each plate is called sea-floor spreading.

The mid-Atlantic Ridge is one of the places where new crust is being formed in this way. The North American and South American Plates are slowly moving away from the Eurasian and African Plates.

Fold mountains and volcanoes

Mid-ocean ridge

Deep ocean trench

Island arc

Crust

Mantle

Plate 1   Plate 2   Plate 3   Plate 4

Subduction zone   Construction zone   Subduction zone

▲ WHERE IS THE EARTH'S CRUST BEING DESTROYED?

Most scientists believe that the area of the earth's surface remains the same. So while material is being added to the crust at the junction of some crustal plates, it is being lost at the junctions of other plates.

As the Atlantic slowly widens, and the Americas move away from Eurasia and Africa, material from the earth's crust is being lost around the edges of the Pacific Ocean.

The boundaries of the crustal plates at the edge of the Pacific are marked by deep ocean trenches roughly twice as deep as the ocean itself. Scientists now believe that these mark areas where the floor of the Pacific Ocean is being dragged very slowly down under the neighboring continental plates.

This type of boundary is called a destructive plate margin. The ocean floor is dragged down at an angle toward the mantle. This process is called subduction.

As subduction occurs, the

solid rock melts. This molten material rises through cracks in the rocks above, forming volcanoes. As the crustal plates slide across each other, earthquakes often occur, and the overriding continental crust is folded and pushed up to form mountains.

Recent evidence of activity at a destructive plate margin was the eruption of Mount St. Helens in the USA. Mount St. Helens is one of an arc of volcanoes caused by the subduction of the San Juan de Fuca Plate beneath the North American Plate.

▶ WHERE IS THE SAN ANDREAS FAULT?

The San Andreas fault is in western California, near the state's Pacific coast. It is named after a lake to the south of the city of San Francisco.

The San Andreas fault and the less famous Fairweather fault in Alaska form the boundary between the Pacific Plate and the North American Plate. The Pacific Plate is slowly rotating anti-clockwise. West of the San Andreas fault, the land is moving north-westward. The result is that a 1,500-mile-long stretch of America from north of San Francisco to the tip of Baja California is being slowly moved along the coast at an average rate of about 2 inches a year. But it moves in a series of jumps, causing earthquakes along the fault. San Francisco was badly damaged by an earthquake in 1906 (shown here), when the fault jumped 21 feet. The next big jump will probably be near Los Angeles, which lies farther south along the fault.

◀ WHERE IS THE GREAT RIFT VALLEY?

The Great Rift Valley is a series of linked rift valleys which stretch for 4,030 miles from north of the River Jordan, via the Dead Sea and the Red Sea, through Ethiopia and East Africa to the coast near the mouth of the Zambezi River.

A rift valley occurs when a narrow strip of the earth's crust sinks between roughly parallel faults. The Great Rift Valley is between 18 and 37 miles wide and has steep fault scarps on each side for most of its length. The Red Sea fills part of its length. Elsewhere there are long, narrow, deep lakes such as Turkana, Mobutu, Tanganyika and Malawi. In East Africa, the route of the Rift Valley splits into two branches, on either side of Lake Victoria. Faulting probably began about 13 million years ago, and earthquakes and volcanic activity have accompanied the subsequent subsidence and uplift.

▶ WHERE WILL THE CONTINENTS BE IN ANOTHER 50 MILLION YEARS?

The map shows where the continents might be *if* they continue to move at their present rate. The shape of the continents will change, as will their locations.

Around 250 million years ago, ancient continents moved together to form one land mass (Pangea) and one vast ocean (Panthalassa). About 150 million years ago Pangea began to split up, and this process continues today. The Pacific Ocean is all that remains of Panthalassa, and is likely to get smaller. The Americas will be pushed farther west, and will separate as the Atlantic Ocean widens. Australia will be farther north; Eurasia farther south and east.

Smaller pieces of land will move, too. California west of the San Andreas fault will be well on its way to join Alaska. Africa will split, making the Mediterranean smaller.

13

◄ WHERE ARE THE OLDEST ROCKS?

The oldest part of a rock that has been dated is some gneiss from the Ameralik Fiord in western Greenland, estimated to be about 3,800 million years old.

Gneiss is a metamorphic rock, one that has been changed by heat and pressure. It is one of many ancient rocks that form Greenland and the neighboring Canadian Shield. These rocks are the ancient base of the North American continent.

The samples were dated by measuring the rate of change of tiny amounts of radioactive rubidium and strontium in the rock.

It is significant that the oldest rocks have been found on a land area, for it shows how long-lasting the lighter rocks of the continents are. In contrast, the oldest known rocks of the ocean floors are only 200 million years old. It is beneath the oceans that the earth's crust is being created and destroyed.

▲ WHERE CAN YOU SEE OVER 1,500 MILLION YEARS OF ROCK STRATA?

The Colorado Desert in the southwestern United States has layers of rock formed over a period of about 1,600 million years. The Colorado River and its tributaries have sliced through these layers in the Grand Canyon and other nearby canyons.

The Grand Canyon area is the only place on earth where geologists can study so many layers of undisturbed rock and an almost perfect sequence of fossils.

The "Granite Gorge" at the bottom of the Grand Canyon is cut into the rocks that form the base of most of North America. These ancient rocks were formed about 1,700 million years ago. They are buried beneath horizontal layers of rocks. At the bottom of the pile is the Tapeats Sandstone, 570 million years old. At the top of the pile, on the rim of the Canyon, is the Kaibab Limestone, about 270 million years old. Layers of more recent rocks have been eroded from the top of the Grand Canyon.

The rocks of the top of the Grand Canyon form the base of Zion Canyon. This canyon is cut into sandstones that are 150 to 200 million years old. The youngest rocks in Zion Canyon form the base of Bryce Canyon where 60 million-year-old shales, sandstones and limestones have been eroded into countless spires. The youngest rocks of the Colorado Plateau are at Brian Head, the plateau's highest point, and are only 37 million years old.

▼ WHERE DO CRYSTALS FORM?

Crystals form either where a solution has evaporated slowly or where molten rock has cooled slowly beneath the surface. The best crystals are those which have the space and the time to form slowly.

You can make salt crystals by leaving seawater (or a strong salt solution) undisturbed to evaporate slowly.

Where a hot mineral solution forces its way into cracks in rocks, and then cools down very slowly, crystals may grow in any spaces left as the solution cools and shrinks. You may find beautiful crystals of quartz or calcite in rocks that have been veined with mineral solutions millions of years ago. Igneous rocks are formed from a variety of molten minerals which cool to form rocks. If the hot rock cools very slowly, the minerals will grow large. Granite is a rock which cooled deep in the earth's crust. If you look at a granite sample you can see crystals of quartz and feldspar.

▲ WHERE ARE DIAMONDS FOUND?

Diamonds were formed deep underground in conditions of intense heat and pressure. The pictures show an uncut diamond and one that has been cut and polished.

Artificial diamonds can be made in factories. Pure carbon is baked under great pressure to over 1,400°C. Natural diamonds probably formed under similar conditions.

Diamonds are thought to have been formed millions of

years ago from carbon which was caught up in molten rock deep in the earth's crust. This molten rock reached the surface in a few places in the form of tube-like "pipes." As it cooled, it turned into a rock called kimberlite. Kimberlite pipes are mined for diamonds in South Africa, Tanzania and Siberia. But many diamonds come from the gravels of rivers which once eroded away kimberlite pipes. Such diamonds are found in many parts of Africa, India, Indonesia, Brazil, Australia and the USSR.

▼ WHERE ARE THE BEST PLACES TO LOOK FOR GOLD?

Gold is found in mineral veins in rocks, or in gravels which have been washed away from areas where gold-bearing rocks have been eroded. Prospectors may pan the gravel in streams for grains of gold, as shown in the photograph.

Gold is sometimes found with quartz veins where extremely hot solutions containing molten gold have cooled in cracks and joints in the rocks. Rich veins have been found in areas of recent volcanic activity, earthquakes and mountain-building, such as the mountains on the western edge of the American continents. Famous gold rushes took place in Alaska, California and the Andes, and in 1980 a rich new find was made in the Chilean Andes.

Placer deposits are those washed down with river gravels or moved by ice. Much of South Africa's gold comes from mines reaching down to ancient gravels which formed a rock called conglomerate.

▼ WHERE IS THE WORLD'S GREATEST MOUNTAIN RANGE?

The greatest mountain range on land is the Himalaya-Karakoram Range to the north of India. It has most of the world's highest peaks.

The Andes of South America are a longer but lower mountain range. There are also great mountain ranges beneath the oceans, the longest of which stretches from the Gulf of Aden to the Gulf of California.

"Himalaya" means "abode of snow" in Sanskrit, an ancient Indian language. This great mountain range stretches about 1,550 miles from east to west and 50 to 93 miles from north to south. Seventy-nine peaks are over 24,600 feet high.

The Himalayas were formed in the last 35 million years at the boundary of two crustal plates, the Indian Plate and the Eurasian Plate. When the edges of these two crustal plates collided, they crumpled to form a great mountain range.

▼ WHERE IS THE LARGEST ACTIVE VOLCANO?

The highest active volcanoes on land are in the Andes, in South America. But even larger volcanoes rise from the floor of the Pacific Ocean and form the islands of Hawaii.

Mauna Loa, on Hawaii, is probably the largest active volcano in the world. It rises 13,681 feet above sea level, but its base is 17,000 feet below sea level. This base is roughly oval in shape: 73 miles long and 53 miles across. So a colossal amount of volcanic material forms this mountain.

The lava from Hawaiian volcanoes (shown here) is very liquid and flows for long distances. Mauna Loa erupts about every 3½ years. Kilauea Crater, southeast of the main volcano, is filled with a red-hot lava lake called Halemaumau, "The Fire Pit."

Volcanoes in the Andes reach higher above sea level than Mauna Loa. Ojos del Salada, on the border of Argentina and Chile, is 22,589 feet high.

▲ WHERE IS THE WORLD'S HIGHEST MOUNTAIN?

Mount Everest is the highest mountain on land: 29,028 feet high. It is in the Himalayas, on the border of Nepal and Tibet.

The height of Mount Everest was discovered in 1852. It was named after Sir George Everest, the Surveyor-General of India at the time. It is called *Sagarmatha* in Nepalese and *Miti Guti Chapu Long-na* in Tibetan.

Like the other high peaks of the Himalayas, Everest is snow-covered all year. Avalanches are common and glaciers fill the valleys. These present great difficulties to climbers, who also face low temperatures, high winds and lack of oxygen.

Although the top of Everest is the highest point of the earth's surface, it is not the tallest mountain when measured from base to peak. Mauna Kea on Hawaii is a total of 32,884 feet tall – only 13,796 feet above sea level but its base is 19,088 feet below the Pacific.

▼ WHERE HAS A VOLCANO GIVEN BIRTH TO AN ISLAND?

The photograph shows Surtsey, an island off the coast of Iceland that was born in a flurry of steam and boiling sea in November 1963. It is just one of many thousands of islands that are volcanoes. Vulcano, an Italian island rising from the Mediterranean Sea, gave its name to all volcanoes.

The mid-Atlantic Ridge is a string of volcanoes down the middle of the Atlantic Ocean. These volcanoes often erupt as new material is added to the earth's crust. The ridge rises above sea level in Iceland, where there are many active volcanoes, lava flows, geysers and hot springs. Tristan da Cunha is another volcano on the same ridge, but far away in the South Atlantic.

The Pacific has many island volcanoes. An arc-shaped pattern of volcanic islands is found near many of the deep-sea trenches, such as the Aleutian Islands. Other volcanoes rise from the ocean floor above "hot spots" beneath the earth's crust. Examples include the Hawaiian Islands in the Pacific and the Azores in the Atlantic.

▶ WHERE WAS THE BIGGEST VOLCANIC ERUPTION?

The biggest explosion in history happened in 1883 when the island of Krakatoa, in Indonesia, was blown to bits. In 1815, another Indonesian volcano, Tambora, produced the most matter discharged in any known eruption.

Krakatoa was an island in the Sunda Straits between Sumatra and Java. Before 1883 it covered 29 square miles. The eruption of 27 August 1883 woke people in Australia and India, 1,860 miles away. Rocks were hurled 34 miles up into the atmosphere and volcanic dust fell on places over 3,100 miles away. Tidal waves caused as much damage and more deaths than the eruption itself. For three years after Krakatoa exploded, the fine dust in the upper atmosphere cooled the weather and caused amazing sunsets in Europe.

Today, a small volcano is growing in the remains of the old volcano.

▼ WHICH VOLCANO DESTROYED AN ANCIENT ROMAN TOWN?

Mount Vesuvius rises above the Bay of Naples in southern Italy. In AD 79 this volcano erupted and buried Pompeii, Herculaneum and other Roman towns.

Mount Vesuvius had been dormant for 800 years. Few people realized that it was a volcano, and those who did thought it was extinct. Fine towns were built on the Bay of Naples, and the rich soil on the slopes of Vesuvius was farmed. Then, on 24 August 79 Mount Vesuvius suddenly erupted. Gases trapped inside built up such pressure that tons of lava, pumice and ash were blown out.

For three days Pompeii was bombarded with pumice and ash. About 16,000 people died. But the ash preserved minute details of Roman life for archaeologists.

Nearby Herculaneum was buried under 40 feet of boiling mud. Vesuvius was blown apart in the eruption. But part of the wall of the old crater still exists.

▼ WHERE IS THE PACIFIC "RING OF FIRE"?

When the world's volcanoes are plotted on a map, the Pacific Ocean appears surrounded by a ring of fiery volcanic activity.

Around the Pacific Ocean there are many active volcanoes. Some of the world's highest volcanoes are in the Andes and the mountains of Central America. Other volcanoes are found in the mountains of the western USA and Alaska. The Aleutians are a chain of volcanic islands. There are more active volcanoes in the Kamchatka Peninsula of the USSR, and in Japan, Papua-New Guinea and New Zealand. In addition, huge volcanoes rise from the Pacific Ocean floor to form Hawaii and other islands.

Most of the volcanoes that ring the Pacific are found quite near the deep sea trenches at the edge of the ocean. They are caused by the destruction of the Pacific Ocean Plate as it disappears beneath the surrounding continental plates.

▲ WHERE HAVE THE STRONGEST EARTHQUAKES OCCURRED?

The strongest earthquakes so far this century have occurred in Colombia (in 1906); San Francisco, USA (1906); China (1920 and 1976); Japan (1923); Assam, India (1950); Kamchatka, USSR (1952); Aleutians (1957); Chile (1960); Alaska (1964).

Earthquakes are usually measured on a scale devised by Charles Richter in 1954. Since 1977, the biggest quakes have been recorded on the Kanamori scale. On this new scale, the strongest earthquake this century occurred at Lebu, in Chile on 22 May 1960. It measured 9.5 on the Kanamori scale. A 186-mile long stretch of the coast sank six feet into the Pacific. Shock waves were felt around the earth for two weeks.

Many serious earthquakes have occurred around the Pacific Ocean. Like volcanoes, they are caused by movement at the edges of crustal plates.

▶ WHERE DOES MUD BOIL?

Boiling mud is one of the side effects of volcanic activity. Hot water and gases from beneath the surface bubble through the mud, so that it looks like heating oatmeal.

Boiling mud is found in a number of volcanic areas of the world. Volcanic gases such as sulfur, which create the heat and boiling effect, usually give the mud a bad odor. But the minerals are thought to promote healing, so mud pools are often health centers.

People visit the Italian island of Vulcano to be coated in hot, smelly mud as a cure for rheumatism. Similar healing centers thrive near the hot mud pools and springs of the volcanic plateau in North Island, New Zealand.

Boiling mud is still found where volcanoes have been inactive for centuries, such as on the West Indian island of St. Lucia. This shows that heat is still coming from deep down, and volcanic activity is not dead.

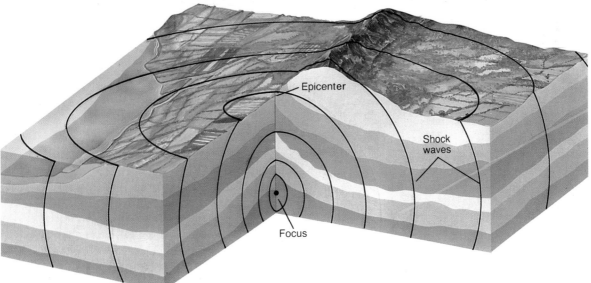

Epicenter

Shock waves

Focus

▲ WHERE IS THE EPICENTER OF AN EARTHQUAKE?

The epicenter of an earthquake is the point on the earth's surface immediately above the place where the movement of the earth's crust has caused shock waves.

Earthquakes occur where rock layers are moving against one another on a fault line. Sudden release of the tension sends out shock waves (called seismic waves) in all directions. The point from which the seismic waves radiate is called the focus. As the diagram shows, the epicenter is at the earth's surface above the focus.

The depth of an earthquake is the distance between the focus and the epicenter. Seismologists (people who study earthquakes) classify earthquakes as shallow if the focus is less than 31 miles beneath the epicenter, and deep if the focus is more than 124 miles below.

As the epicenter is the closest point to the focus, it feels the shocks first and usually suffers the most damage. Surface waves radiate out from the epicenter and damage surrounding areas.

Deep earthquakes are felt over great distances. The 1897 earthquake in Assam, northern India, was one of the deepest on record. Tremors were felt in Rome, Strasbourg and Edinburgh.

Shallow earthquakes may cause great damage near the epicenter but are less noticeable farther away. The 1960 earthquake at Agadir, Morocco, flattened the city center, yet less than a mile away there was little damage.

19

▲ WHERE ARE THE WORLD'S HOTTEST PLACES?

The highest shade temperature on record is 58°C in September 1922 at Al'Aziziyah in the Sahara Desert in Libya. Nearly as hot was the 56.7°C recorded in Death Valley in California, in July 1913.

You might expect the hottest places to be on the equator. Although equatorial lands are hot all year, they are also very cloudy. The hot deserts are near the Tropics where the sun is overhead in midsummer. Because there is very little rain, there is very little cloud, so it is sunny and hot all day.

The eastern Sahara has more sunshine than anywhere else: sunshine has been recorded for 4,300 hours in a year. That is an average of 11 hours 47 minutes per day. So it is not surprising that the highest temperature on record occurred in the Sahara.

The picture shows Death Valley, also a desert, where temperatures up to 50°C in summer are not unusual.

▲ WHERE ARE THE WORLD'S COLDEST PLACES?

The coldest temperatures are recorded in winter in Antarctica. In July 1983, Russian scientists measured a new record low of −89.2°C.

Until modern weather stations were set up in Antarctica, the coldest temperatures were recorded in Siberia: −68°C was recorded at Verkhoyansk in 1892. Verkhoyansk holds the record for experiencing the greatest temperature range: from a coldest winter temperature of −68°C to a hottest summer temperature of 36.7°C.

The Arctic "cold pole" is some way from the North Pole because of the surrounding Arctic Ocean. Seas have a moderating effect on the climate of coastal areas. Verkhoyansk is inland from the Arctic Ocean, and a long way from any other sea. The huge land mass of Eurasia heats up quickly in summer to give surprisingly high temperatures even in the far north, but it loses its heat quickly in winter.

▲ WHERE DOES FROST COME FROM?

Frost is small crystals of ice which cling to any surface such as twigs, blades of grass or windows. It forms when the temperature is low enough for water vapor in the air to condense as ice instead of as water droplets.

The air around us always contains some water vapor. Cold air can hold less water vapor than warm air. At the end of a warm day the air will cool down. If the air is moist and still, some of the water vapor will condense as mist or dew. If the temperature falls below freezing, ice crystals will form instead of water droplets. A coating of ice crystals is called frost.

Frost is especially likely on a clear calm night. If there is no cloud cover to act as a blanket over the surface of the earth, heat will radiate back into the atmosphere very quickly, and temperatures will fall fast. Because cold air tends to fall, frost may occur in hollows and valley bottoms and not on the hill slopes above.

Very high rainfall occurs when warm, moist winds are forced to rise. As the air cools, the water vapor condenses as rain.

Cherrapunji clings to a hillside in Assam, in northeast India. It faces the full force of the monsoon winds as they sweep north from the Indian Ocean in July. As the warm, wet winds rise toward the Himalayas, torrential rain falls for a few weeks. The photograph shows a dense rain forest in Assam.

The Hawaiian mountains are wet all year. They are in the path of the Northeast Trade Winds which pick up moisture from the vast Pacific Ocean. This causes the record rainfall on Mount Wai-'ale-'ale. It has 350 rainy days a year, and has the highest average annual rainfall on earth: 37.5 feet.

▲ WHERE ARE THE WETTEST PLACES ON EARTH?

Cherrapunji, in India, holds the record for the most rain in one month: 30.5 feet in July 1861. It also had the most rain in a year: 86.8 feet in the year up to 31 July 1861. Mount Wai-'ale-'ale in Hawaii has the most rainy days (350 a year), and the highest average annual rainfall.

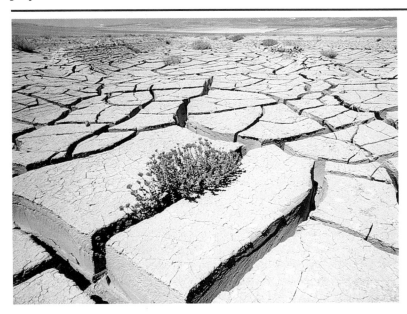

air descends and is therefore warm and dry. There is little cloud, so the sunny days are intensely hot, but the starry nights can be cold.

The Atacama Desert is exceptionally dry, but rainfall is very low in all desert areas. Cairo, in the eastern Sahara, averages 1.12 inches a year. Bahrain, on the edge of the Arabian Desert, has 3.2 inches. But average rainfall figures for deserts can be confusing: there may be heavy storms on a few days in some years, and almost continuous drought in others.

Not all the dry parts of the earth are also hot. Large areas of Central Asia are sheltered by mountains from any rain-bearing winds. Yet deserts such as the Gobi are very cold in winter. The Polar lands are also very dry – although the moisture that does fall accumulates as snow.

▲ WHERE IS THE DRIEST PLACE ON EARTH?

The photograph shows the Atacama Desert in northern Chile, where the first rain for 400 years fell in 1971. All deserts are dry, but the Atacama is the driest.

The Atacama Desert is hemmed in between the Pacific Ocean and the Andes mountains. The Andes shut out all winds from the east. Like the other hot deserts of the world, the Atacama lies astride one of the Tropics where air pressure is high. The

▼ WHERE ARE THE WORLD'S LONGEST GLACIERS?

Eight of the world's ten longest glaciers are in Antarctica. The longest is the Lambert-Fisher Ice Passage, which has a total length of 319 miles.

Petermann's Glacier in Greenland is the largest glacier in the northern hemisphere, and extends 25 miles out to sea.

The largest glaciers are fed with ice from the great ice sheets covering Antarctica and Greenland. Greenland has the fastest-moving glacier: the Quarayaq advances at 67-79 feet a day.

Spectacular glaciers are found elsewhere in the world. The longest Himalayan glacier is the Siachen (47 miles long) in the Karakoram Range. Also in the Himalayas, the Hispar and Biafo Glaciers join to form an ice passage 76 miles long.

Among the world's twenty longest glaciers are those in North America (in Alaska), Asia (in the Pamirs), in New Zealand and in the Alps.

▼ WHERE ARE THE WORLD'S BIGGEST EXPANSES OF ICE?

Just over 10 percent of the land surface of the world is permanently covered by ice. Most of the world's ice (87 percent) is in Antarctica. The Arctic has 12.5 percent (mainly covering Greenland), and the rest is found in the glaciers which exist on every continent.

Antarctica is covered almost completely by the world's

- ■ Ice caps
- ■ Permanent pack ice
- ■ Winter extent of pack ice
- ■ Permafrost

Siberia

Iceland

Greenland

ARCTIC

ANTARCTIC

largest ice sheet and only a few edges of the shore are exposed. In all, there are 5,250,000 square miles of ice. The thickest ice recorded was 15,669 feet in depth.

The North Pole is an ocean area, and the largest area of land ice is on Greenland where the ice sheet covers 656,400 square miles. It is about 9,843 feet thick at its center.

The total amount of ice outside the polar regions is very small. The largest expanse is in Iceland: 3,398 square miles.

▲ WHERE IS PERMAFROST FOUND?

Permafrost is permanently frozen ground. It is found beneath permanent ice and snow. It is also found in large areas around the Arctic Ocean where the snow melts in summer but only the top few centimeters of the soil thaw.

Permafrost covers the whole of Antarctica. In the Arctic, permafrost is shallowest near the coast and deepest inland where the weather is coldest.

Permafrost 4,495 feet deep has been found in Siberia.

In summer, when the snow melts and the topsoil thaws, water cannot drain into the frozen ground below. The whole surface is marshy.

It is difficult to build on permafrost. Heated buildings have to be insulated from the ground beneath, else they defrost the soil and sink into the mud. Permafrost is also a great hindrance to oil-drilling and mining. But it has preserved the remains of ancient animals, such as woolly mammoths.

▼ WHERE ARE THE BIGGEST ICEBERGS FOUND?

The icebergs with the biggest area are the tabular icebergs that break away from Antarctica. The largest ever seen was over 12,000 square miles (bigger than Belgium). The tallest icebergs break away from Greenland. The tallest ever seen was 548 feet above the water.

The iceberg with the largest area was seen in the South Pacific in 1956. The huge icebergs in this area have broken away from the Ross Ice Shelf. There, the Antarctic ice sheet extends out over the sea in an ice shelf as large as France. Its ice cliffs tower up to 164 feet above the sea. Along its 403-mile front it cracks with the rise and fall of the tide. Enormous icebergs break loose and float northward into the Pacific.

The very tall Arctic icebergs are especially dangerous as eight-ninths of the ice is hidden beneath the sea.

ARCTIC ICEBERGS

TABULAR ICEBERGS

▲ WHERE DO ICEBERGS MELT?

Icebergs gradually melt as they float away from the polar lands. But how long it takes will depend on the size of the iceberg and the temperature of the sea.

Melting icebergs have been seen very close to tropical waters. In 1935, an Arctic iceberg was recorded at latitude 28½°N in the North Atlantic. And in 1894 a ship recorded an iceberg in the Atlantic at latitude 26½°S.

As icebergs drift away from the polar regions they are melted by the sun and by warmer water. Waves and rain erode them further. An iceberg may actually break apart while drifting, and if this disturbs its balance it may roll over. As an iceberg melts, the rocks in the ice sink to the sea bed.

Cold ocean currents carry icebergs far away from their point of origin. When the cold Labrador Current continues farther south than usual, it brings Arctic icebergs into the busy North Atlantic shipping route.

▼ WHERE ARE CREVASSES FOUND?

Crevasses are cracks in the ice of glaciers and ice sheets. They are often quite narrow, but extremely deep and dangerous, especially if hidden by a thin crust of frozen snow.

The great mass of ice in a glacier or ice sheet moves slowly downhill. But the surface layers are always rigid and brittle. Different parts of a glacier move at different rates: the surface moves faster than the base, and the center of the surface moves faster than the sides.

The different rates of flow create tensions in the ice and cause cracks in the surface layers. Whenever a glacier flows around a bend or over a hump, or changes its speed for some other reason, crevasses and pressure ridges form.

At the head of a mountain glacier there is an especially deep crevasse called the Bergschrund. This forms where the glacier ice is pulling away from the permanent snow on the mountain slope.

Movement of glacier

Slope of land

Crevasses

▼ WHERE IS THE GREATEST OCEAN CURRENT?

The greatest ocean current is the West Wind Drift (also called the Antarctic Circumpolar Current). Its cold waters originate near the Antarctic and encircle that continent. The current is driven along by strong westerly winds.

The West Wind Drift varies in width from 124 to 186 miles. Its surface flow is less than .62 mile an hour. Measurements made in Drake Passage, where the current is squeezed between South America and Antarctica, recorded a flow of water at nearly 10,000 million cubic feet per second – three times the greatest flow of the Gulf Stream.

The West Wind Drift is driven along by the strong westerly winds of the Southern Hemisphere. These are called the Roaring Forties because they blow at latitudes 40°-50°S. There are few land obstacles this far south to either wind or ocean current. Here there are some of the roughest seas and fiercest gales.

▼ WHERE ARE THE DOLDRUMS?

The doldrums is a name given by early sailors to a zone at the equator where winds are often light, their direction uncertain and where sailing ships were often becalmed.

For sailors in sailing ships, the doldrums were a great contrast to the trade winds which blow steadily in the zone between the Tropics and the equator. The Northeast and Southeast Trade Winds converge on the equator where pressure is low and the air rises.

Because the air rises at the equator there is plenty of rain. Sudden squalls and thunderstorms occur frequently, even though, in general, winds blow along the surface lightly. Sailing in such conditions is difficult because the boat is not carried along in any particular direction.

The exact location of the doldrums moves with the seasons. In June they are about 5° north of the equator, and in December they are about 5° south.

▼ WHERE IS THE GULF STREAM?

The Gulf Stream is a warm ocean current which begins in the Gulf of Mexico and flows across the North Atlantic toward Europe.

The Gulf Stream bursts into the Atlantic through the Straits of Florida, between the USA and Cuba. It flows close to the coast of America as far as Cape Hatteras and then continues northeast toward Europe. In the open ocean it is driven along by the westerly winds.

The Gulf Stream is a meandering current about 62 miles wide. Its average speed is less than .62 mile an hour. To the north of the Gulf Stream there is a very sudden change to cold water. And as it is only a surface current, the water temperature cools rapidly below 1,148 feet.

The warm water of the Gulf Stream is vital to northern Europe. Ports are ice-free and the weather is warm enough for farming much farther north in Europe than in eastern Canada on the opposite side of the Atlantic.

▶ WHERE IS THE ABYSSAL PLAIN?

"Abyss" usually means the lowest depth of the oceans. The abyssal plain is the deep ocean floor. As the diagram shows, it lies nearly 4,000 meters beneath the ocean surface. Large areas are almost flat and featureless. The abyssal plain has been called "the smoothest surface on earth." But in places the plain is broken up by deep chasms and sea mountains.

The abyssal plain covers about two-thirds of the ocean floor. It begins at the foot of the steep continental slope. Here, sediments have slumped off the slope and been dumped by muddy currents. Away from the continental slope, the layer of sediments on the abyssal plain thins out and its slope becomes almost level.

Features such as undersea volcanoes and deep ocean trenches break up the surface of the abyssal plain at the margins of crustal plates. There are also isolated seamounts, but few reach the surface to form islands.

Continental shelf

Metres
1000
2000
3000
Abyssal plain
4000
5000
6000
7000
8000
9000
10,000
Deep ocean trench
11,000

◀ WHERE IS THE DEEPEST PART OF THE OCEAN?

The deepest part of the ocean was found in 1951 by the survey ship *Challenger*. Echo soundings showed that part of the Mariana Trench, south of Japan, is 10,900 meters deep. In 1960 the US Navy bathyscaphe *Trieste* descended to the bottom of the Challenger Deep.

The Mariana Trench is one of many deep-sea trenches around the edges of the Pacific Ocean. These V-shaped trenches are parallel to a continent or line of islands.

A deep-sea trench plunges down from the abyssal plain. It may be 50-100 kilometers wide at the top, but only a few kilometers wide at the bottom. Most are found in the Pacific, but they also occur in the Caribbean, the South Atlantic and the Indian Ocean.

Deep-sea trenches mark places where the ocean floor is being subducted beneath a continental plate. Scientists are studying sediments in the deep trenches, which might one day be used for dumping dangerous waste materials.

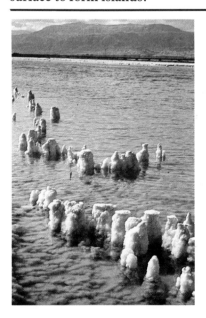

◀ WHICH SEA IS THE SALTIEST?

The Dead Sea, on the borders of Israel and Jordan, is the world's saltiest sea. It is over ten times saltier than the average ocean.

The Dead Sea has no exit. Most of its water comes from the north, in the River Jordan. Mineral springs at the bottom of the Dead Sea, and around its shores, add to the salts in the water. The climate is very hot and dry, so an enormous amount of water is lost by evaporation. Salts in the water are therefore very concentrated. They are extracted in large evaporation pans. The picture shows natural salt deposits in the Dead Sea.

The shores of the Dead Sea are the lowest exposed point on the earth's surface: 1,289 feet below sea level.

To the south is the Red Sea, the saltiest part of the open sea. Here, too, the salt is concentrated because so much water evaporates in the hot sun and so little is added from the surrounding desert.

▼ WHERE IS THE LARGEST ARCHIPELAGO?

An archipelago is a sea studded with islands. The word was first used for the Aegean Sea with its many Greek islands. The largest archipelago is in southeast Asia where thousands of islands make up the countries of Indonesia, eastern Malaysia and the Philippines.

The country of Indonesia is made up of over 13,000 islands of which about 3,000 are inhabited. The islands stretch over 3,100 miles from west of the Malay Peninsula to New Guinea. Many of the islands in Indonesia are volcanoes. They form a great arc to the north of a deep-sea trench called the Java Trench.

Indonesia shares two of its islands with two other countries. Eastern Malaysia is part of the island of Borneo, and Papua-New Guinea shares an island with West Irian.

There are over 7,000 islands in the Philippines, although more than 90 percent of the land area consists of just the eleven largest islands.

▼ WHERE DO TIDAL BORES OCCUR?

A tidal bore is a high wave which travels up an estuary as the tide comes in. Such bores are found only where there is a big tidal range and a funnel-shaped estuary.

As the tide rises in a river estuary, it is held back by the shallow water and the out-flowing river current. This causes the water to pile up and move up the river like a large breaking wave.

The most remarkable bore is on the River Ch'ient'ang'kian which flows into the Bay of Hangchow (Hangzhou) in China. Each spring tide, the bore is 24.6 feet high, and travels at 14.8 miles an hour. It can be heard coming 13 or more miles away!

The tidal bore with the greatest volume flows up the Canal do Norte, the main exit of the River Amazon. One of the fastest tidal bores flows up the River Hooghly, which is a branch of the River Ganges.

In contrast, the tidal bore on the River Severn in England is only over 3 feet high.

▲ WHERE ARE THE WORLD'S HIGHEST TIDES?

The greatest rise and fall of the tide is recorded in the Bay of Fundy, between New Brunswick and Nova Scotia provinces in eastern Canada. The average spring tide range is 47.5 feet, though tidal ranges of up to 53 feet are recorded.

The tides of the Atlantic Ocean are funnelled into the narrow Bay of Fundy to produce the largest tidal range. This enormous range creates a tidal bore in the bay, even though it is not the estuary of a major river. The tidal flow enriches the marine life in the water, and the Bay is a haven for wading birds.

In Europe, the Rance estuary in northern France has a large tidal range. It is the site of the world's first tidal power station.

Unexpected high tides can cause great damage. They are usually the result of tidal surges, caused by very high winds and low air pressure at the same time as the expected high tide.

▼ WHERE IS THE LONGEST REEF IN THE WORLD?

The Great Barrier Reef, off the northeast coast of Australia, is the world's longest coral reef. It stretches for over 1,240 miles from near Papua to the center of the Queensland coast.

Coral reefs can only form in tropical seas where the water is warm and shallow enough for the coral polyps to flourish. Like many other reefs, the Great Barrier Reef plunges into water which is too deep for corals to survive today. But sea level was probably much lower in the past when the reef first began to form.

The Great Barrier Reef lies between 28 and 40 miles off the Australian coast. In the north it is only 9-12 miles wide, but in the south the reef area extends up to 200 miles out to sea. There are only about ten safe passages through the reef, so it is a perilous area to navigate.

More than 340 varieties of coral have been identified on the reef. They present an incredible array of colors and shapes and are the homes of many beautiful fish and other sea creatures. Recently, parts of the reef have been destroyed by the Crown of Thorns starfish which sucks the living polyps off the hard coral skeletons.

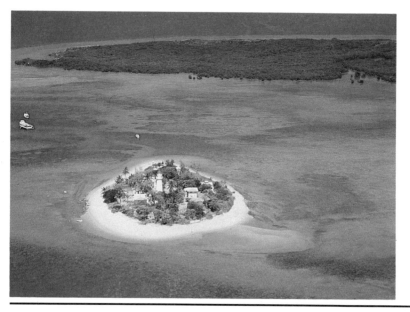

▼ WHERE ARE FIORDS FOUND?

Fiords are long, narrow, steep-sided inlets of the sea. They were made by glaciers **which deepened the valleys along which they flowed. After the glaciers disappeared, their U-shaped valleys were flooded by the sea to form fiords.**

Fiords are found on mountainous coasts which have been eroded by glaciers. The fiords of Norway are famous and are among the longest in the world. Sogne Fiord is 113 miles long from the open sea to the head of Lusterfiord. Its average width is 3 miles. Like most fiords, it is exceptionally deep, but becomes shallower toward the coast. At its deepest point, Sogne Fiord is 4,085 feet deep.

Even longer is the Nordvest Fiord arm of Scoresby Sound in eastern Greenland. This fiord is 194 miles long.

Fiords are also found along the coast of Iceland, the Pacific coast of Canada and Alaska, in southern Chile and in South Island, New Zealand. The picture shows a village at the head of a Norwegian fiord.

◄ WHICH IS THE LONGEST RIVER?

The three longest rivers in the world are the Nile in Africa: 4,135 miles long; the Amazon in South America: 3,998 miles; and the Mississippi-Missouri in North America: 3,700 miles.

Different experts give different lengths for these great rivers. This is because it is not easy to say exactly where a river begins and where it ends. All have many tributaries, and there are many channels in their deltas.

Does the Nile begin in Lake Victoria, as some books say? The farthest source of the Nile is the Luvironzo in Burundi, which flows into the Kagera and then into Lake Victoria.

The farthest source of the Amazon was discovered in Peru in 1953. But where does the river end? The Canal do Norte is usually classed as the main exit. But the Rio Para is also navigable, and if this counts as an exit, then the Amazon is 4,185 miles long.

► WHICH IS THE LARGEST RIVER?

The Amazon River is larger than the Nile River. The Amazon drains nearly twice as big an area. It contains far more water, and boats can travel much farther upstream.

The two major tributaries of the Nile, the White Nile and the Blue Nile, begin in areas with quite high rainfall. But for most of its course the Nile flows through desert where little water is added and a lot of water evaporates.

Consequently, the flow of the Nile is low for a major river: an average discharge of 110,000 cubic feet per second. All the world's major rivers, except the Murray-Darling in Australia, have a greater flow.

The River Amazon carries a greater volume of water than any other river: its average discharge is over six million cubic feet per second. Its many long tributaries drain an area of nearly three million square miles, most of which receives heavy rain all year through.

◄ WHERE ARE THE HIGHEST WATERFALLS?

The highest falls in the world are the Angel Falls on the Carrao River, a tributary of the Caroni River, in Venezuela, South America. The total fall of water is 3,212 feet; the longest single drop is 2,648 feet.

The Angel Falls are one of several very high waterfalls in this part of Venezuela, most of which are unmeasured and unnamed. They occur where rivers flow over the edge of a high, steep-sided plateau.

The Angel Falls have long been known to the local Indians who call them Cherun-Meru. Europeans first saw them in 1910. They were then rediscovered in 1937 by an American pilot named Jimmy Angel who crash-landed nearby.

The world's second highest falls are the Tugela Falls in Natal, South Africa. The Tugela River drops 3,107 feet at the falls. In Norway, the Utigard Falls carry water from the melting Jostedal Glacier 2,625 feet into Nesdal.

► WHERE WERE THE WORST FLOODS RECORDED?

Some of the world's worst floods have occurred when the Hwang-ho River in China has burst its banks. Floods in 1931 killed over 3,500,000 people.

Hwang-ho means "Yellow River" and it is the muddiest river in the world. It flows for 2,976 miles through northern China and carries over 1,500 million tons of silt. About a quarter of this silt is dumped near the mouth of the river, to raise the river bed and alter the course of the river channel. For thousands of years dikes have been built to prevent flooding but when the dikes burst disaster occurs.

The main flood season is from July to September, when most of the rain falls. But there are problems in springtime, too, when the southern part of the river thaws while the great loop to the north is still iced up. Sluice gates on the Hwang-ho, like those shown in the picture, are now used for flood control and irrigation.

◄ WHERE IS THE LARGEST LAKE?

The world's largest lake is the Caspian Sea, between Iran and the USSR. Although it is called a sea, it is not connected with the oceans, but is a very large inland lake. Its total area is 143,553 square miles.

The surface of the Caspian Sea is 92 feet below sea level, and the deepest point of the lake is an additional 3,215 feet down.

The Volga and Ural rivers both flow into the Caspian. No river flows out. The lake is in a desert area, so a lot of water evaporates and the water is very salty. As more river water is used for irrigation and industry, so less water reaches the Caspian. The world's largest lake is getting smaller.

The largest freshwater lake is Lake Superior, between the USA and Canada. It covers 31,795 square miles. Lake Superior does have an exit: into Lake Huron and the other Great Lakes and then to the Atlantic via the St. Lawrence River.

► WHERE IS THE HIGHEST LAKE?

The highest lake in the world is an unnamed glacial lake near Mount Everest which lies at 19,291 feet above sea level. Tibet's largest lake, Nam Tso is 15,020 feet above sea level. The world's highest navigable lake is Lake Titicaca (shown here), on the border of Peru and Bolivia. It is 12,503 feet above sea level and is navigated by lake steamers.

The total area of Lake Titicaca is about 3,200 square miles, and its maximum depth is 1,214 feet. The lake receives water from several mountain rivers of the Andes. Its water drains south to Lake Poopo, and then disappears into the dry *altiplano* (high plain).

The land around Lake Titicaca is bleak and treeless. Llamas and vicunas graze on the coarse grass. Totoro reeds grow in the lake and are used by the local Indians to make reed fishing boats, houses and even the islands on which they live.

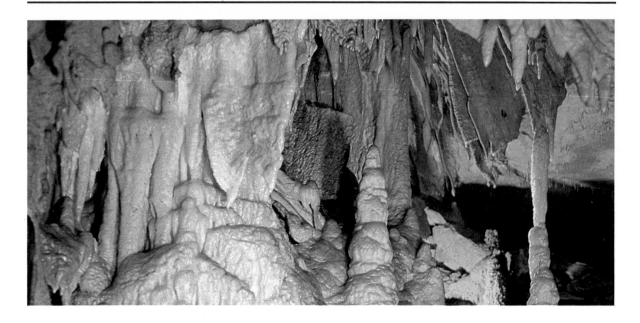

▲ WHERE IS THE BIGGEST CAVE?

The largest single cavern in the world is the Sarawak Chamber, in Sarawak, Eastern Malaysia. It was discovered in 1980.

The largest cave system in the world is under the Mammoth Cave National Park in the state of Kentucky.

Sarawak is part of Eastern Malaysia and is on the island of Borneo in Southeast Asia. The Sarawak Chamber is under the Gunung Mulu National Park. It was surveyed in 1980 and found to be 2,297 feet long, an average of 984 feet wide, and at least 230 feet high.

At Mammoth Cave National Park (see photograph), there is a maze of caves and passageways at different levels. The Mammoth Cave system itself is 190 miles long. Only 2½ miles from the entrance to Mammoth Caves is the entrance to Flint Ridge Caves. In 1972, Mrs. P. Crowther discovered an underground route linking the two cave systems.

▲ WHERE IS THE DEEPEST CAVE?

The deepest cave found so far is the Gouffre Jean Bernard Cave in the French Alps. In 1982, a team of French spelunkers reached a depth of 4,900 feet.

On a five-day expedition in 1982, the Groupe Speleo Vulcain set a new world depth record for spelunkers. Their route down included a dive through a sump 131 feet long which led them into a new series of descending passages. The final cave was measured as 4,900 feet deep.

France has other very deep caves. The Gouffre Berger Caves near Grenoble are .68 miles deep. Gouffre de la Pierre Saint-Martin in the Pyrenees is now known to be 4,429 feet deep.

Snezhnaya Cave in the USSR is now claimed to be the second deepest cave. Explorers have reached a depth of 4,429 feet. They could feel a current of air coming through the rubble at the bottom, and hope to find another passage descending even farther.

▲ WHERE ARE THE LARGEST STALACTITES AND STALAGMITES?

Stalactites hang down from cave roofs. The largest is in Spain. Stalagmites grow up from cave floors. The largest is in France.

Stalactites and stalagmites grow in caves where water saturated with calcium carbonate drips from the cave roof. The deposits build up slowly, so large formations have been undisturbed for thousands of years.

The largest stalactite is a wall-supported column which hangs down 194 feet from the roof of the Cueva de Nerja, east of Malaga in Spain. The huge cave was discovered in 1959 by a shepherd boy looking for his ball. It is now an underground auditorium for concerts and ballets.

The longest free-hanging stalactite hangs down 23 feet in the *Poll an Ionain* cave in County Clare, Ireland.

La Grande Stalagmite in Aven Armand cave in France is the world's tallest. It stands 95 feet high.

▶ WHERE ARE THE LARGEST SAND DUNES?

The highest measured sand dunes are found in central Algeria, in the Sahara Desert. They stand up to 1,410 feet high.

Only about a tenth of the Sahara Desert is covered with wind-blown sand. The rest is gravel plains, plateaus and mountains. Most of the sand is found in 25 large sand seas, called ergs. These are quite distinct from the surrounding sand-free desert.

The highest dunes are found in the sand sea of Isaouane-n-Tifernine to the north of the Hoggar mountains. The Sahara's largest area of sand dunes is the Grand Erg Oriental, on the border of Algeria and Tunisia. This sand sea covers about 200,000 square miles.

The world's largest area of sand dunes is Rub'-al-Khali, "the Empty Quarter," in the Arabian Desert. It covers about 250,970 square miles of southern Saudi Arabia. The central sand mountains rise to 820 feet.

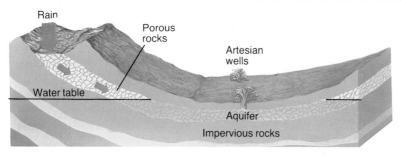

▲ WHERE IS ARTESIAN WATER FOUND?

Artesian water is underground water which rises to the surface under natural pressure. The name comes from Artois in France, **where many wells have been dug to reach artesian water in the underlying chalk.**

The diagram shows how an artesian basin can form. Rain falling on the higher land can flow through the layers of porous rocks. Beneath the low land, the porous rocks are sandwiched between impervious layers. The water-bearing layer is called an aquifer.

In the lowland, a well dug through the top impervious layer will reach the aquifer below. Because the water table (the top of the underground water) is higher than the top of the well, the water will gush to the surface under its own pressure.

The Great Artesian Basin of Australia is the world's largest.

◀ WHERE ARE DESERTS BEING CREATED?

On the edges of some of the earth's natural deserts, the environment is being upset by poor farming methods and mismanagement.

Semi-desert areas have fragile soils and difficult climates. Several good years are often followed by several bad years. In the good years, farmers may extend the cultivated areas, or increase their flocks and herds, and dig more wells. But in a series of dry years crops fail, animals exhaust the pasture, the bare soil is eroded, and many wells dry up. Such problems created the "dust bowl" during the 1930s, and extended the Sahara Desert in the 1970s.

The problem of finding enough fuel for cooking has denuded large areas of semi-desert of all trees and bushes. This makes the soil more prone to erosion. Some areas have been transformed by large irrigation projects, but poor water management can harm the soil. Then, large areas may revert to desert.

**The Netherlands is one of
the smallest countries in
Europe. Yet half its land area
is the result of reclaiming
land from marshes, lakes and
sea.**

The Netherlands lies in the
delta area formed by the Rivers
Rhine, Meuse (Maas) and
Scheldt. Most of the land is
below 98 feet, and half the
total area below high-tide
level.

    The areas of reclaimed land
are called polders. They are
surrounded by dikes (banks) to
keep out flood water, and
crisscrossed by drainage
ditches. The water was once
removed by wind pumps, but
diesel pumps are used now.

    Major modern reclamation

schemes include the Zuider
Zee and Delta Projects. The
Zuider Zee was closed off from
the North Sea by a 20-mile-
long dam in 1932. The former
bay was transformed into the
freshwater Lake Ijssel and 873
square miles of new land in five

huge polders. The Delta
Project involved damming all
but two exits of the Rhine,
Maas and Scheldt. This
scheme protects land from
floods and created a freshwater
reservoir and 58 square miles
of new land.

**Only a fifth of the earth's
land surface is densely
populated, so there are still
plenty of remote places. The
remotest inhabited land is
Tristan da Cunha, a volcanic
island in the South Atlantic.
The nearest inhabited land is
over 1,240 miles away.**

Four-fifths of the earth's land
surface is too dry, too cold, too
mountainous or too densely
forested to support many
people. The most sparsely
populated continent is
Antarctica, which has no
permanent settlement. The
most sparsely populated
country is Greenland.

    The remotest island is
Bouvet Island, an uninhabited
Norwegian dependency in the
South Atlantic. The nearest
land is 1,054 miles away, and

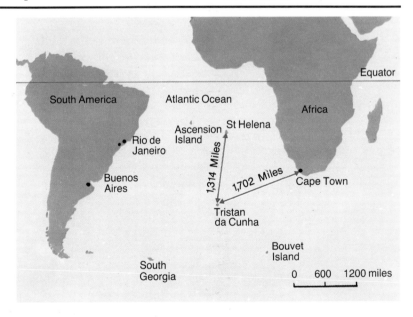

that is the uninhabited coast of
Antarctica.

    The remotest inhabited
island, Tristan da Cunha,
covers just 38 square miles. Its
nearest inhabited land is the
island of St. Helena, 1,314
miles to the northeast.

    In 1961 Tristan da Cunha

erupted and all its inhabitants
were evacuated, but they
returned in 1963. Although the
island looks lonely, they are
happy there. Loneliness is
often worse in great cities than
in remote places.

▲ WHERE IS THE LARGEST ARTIFICIAL LAKE?

The artificial lake with the greatest area is Lake Volta in Ghana, West Africa. The Bratsk Reservoir on the Angara River in the USSR holds the greatest volume of water in an artificial lake.

In 1965, the Akosombo Dam was completed across the Volta River. The dam is built at the southern end of a gorge, and produces hydroelectric power.

Lake Volta began to build up behind the dam in the valley of the Volta River and its main headwaters, the Black Volta and the White Volta. Altogether the lake now covers 3,276 square miles and its shoreline is 4,495 miles long. Villagers had to move from the flooded area to the new shoreline, where they began a fishing industry.

Lake Volta is large but fairly shallow. In places, the remains of flooded forests can still be seen. Its total volume is 36 cubic miles — compared to 40 cubic miles for the USSR's Bratsk Reservoir.

▲ WHERE IS THE BIGGEST MAN-MADE HOLE ON EARTH?

The largest modern quarry, excavated by machine, is Bingham Canyon Copper Mine in Utah, pictured above. It covers 2.8 square miles and is 2,539 feet deep.

The "Big Hole" of Kimberley in South Africa is an old diamond mine which was dug out last century by thousands of miners working with only picks and shovels. It is about 1,640 feet in diameter and nearly 1,312 feet deep.

In 1871 diamonds were found on a farm which became the site of Kimberley Mine. By 1872 more than 3,500 men claimed patches of land where they could dig for diamonds. As they dug out the pipe of kimberlite rock, they made a huge hole. Over 25 million tons of rock were dug out, yielding about three tons of diamonds.

Open mining stopped when rock falls became too frequent. The mine closed in 1915 and is now half full of water.

▲ WHERE DOES ACID RAIN OCCUR?

All rain is very slightly acid, but over the industrial areas of North America and Europe the rain is more acid because it absorbs waste gases which pollute the atmosphere.

Rainwater reacts with the carbon dioxide in the air to become a very dilute carbonic acid. This weak acid can dissolve limestone, which is an alkaline rock.

Rain can also react with the waste gases emitted into the air by factories, power stations and cars. Such gases may be carried great distances by winds and then fall as dilute sulfuric acid and nitric acid, often on areas far away from the source of pollution. This is called acid rain because its acidity is artificially high.

Acid rain increases the erosion of rocks and building materials, especially limestone. Lakes and streams are slowly poisoned, threatening wildlife. The face of the statue shown in the photograph above has been eaten away by acid rain.

33

◀ WHERE IS RICE GROWN?

Rice provides food for more people than any other cereal crop in the world. It is the basic food crop in much of southern and eastern Asia.

Rice needs hot weather and plenty of water. The water may come from heavy rain, such as the monsoon rains of Asia, or from irrigation. Rice needs flat land, because the water level in the fields must be carefully controlled. Many hillsides in Asia are terraced to get enough flat land. Some terraces are hundreds of years old.

The seedlings are grown in a "nursery" bed and then transplanted to the flooded paddyfields. After four to five months the rice is ready for harvest and the water is released.

Rice is now grown in many hot, wet parts of the world apart from Asia. Mechanized rice fields in the USA and southern Europe grow rice for export. Rice is also an important food crop in Egypt, West Africa, Madagascar and parts of South America.

▶ WHERE DOES COTTON COME FROM?

The cotton thread we sew with or weave into cloth is spun from fibers in the cotton boll. This is the seed pod of the cotton plant.

The cotton bush is an annual plant. It grows quickly and flowers, then small green seedpods develop. The seeds inside the cotton boll are surrounded by a mass of fine hairs. When the boll is ripe, it bursts open and the soft white cotton can be picked.

Once the cotton crop is harvested, it has to be ginned. This process separates the cotton fiber from the seeds so that the fibers can be cleaned, carded and spun.

Cotton was a major crop in the southeastern United States where slaves worked the plantations. Nearly a fifth of the world's cotton is still produced here. Egypt and Sudan also export cotton. It is important too in parts of East Africa, India and Pakistan, China and parts of South America.

▶ WHERE IS TEA GROWN?

The tea we drink is made from the crushed leaves of an evergreen bush which grows in hot, damp climates. It seems to thrive at high altitudes, up to 7,546 feet, in tropical areas.

Tea was first brought to Europe from China. As the drink became fashionable, plantations of tea bushes were planted by the Dutch in Indonesia and by the British in India and Sri Lanka. Now tea plantations are also found in Japan, in East Africa and on hillsides in parts of the Soviet Union.

The tea plant needs a warm climate with plenty of moisture and a rich, well-drained soil. On tea plantations, the bush is pruned to a maximum height of five feet so it is easy to pick. The young leaves at the tops of the stems are picked. These are taken to a factory on the plantation where they are spread out to wither. They are then rolled and left to ferment. Heating and drying seals in the flavor and the tea is packed for export.

▶ WHERE DOES RUBBER COME FROM?

Natural rubber is made from latex, which is found under the bark of the rubber tree. This tree is a native of the Amazon rain forest and grows in hot, wet equatorial conditions.

Amazon Indians first collected latex from trees to make a type of rubber. Charles Goodyear discovered how to harden rubber in 1842. When bicycles and cars became popular there was a great demand for rubber and the Amazon became a boom area.

The rubber tree was introduced to Southeast Asia via London's botanical gardens at Kew. Plantations in Malaysia and Indonesia have supplied much of the world's rubber. Smaller amounts come from Zaire and West Africa.

The bark of the rubber tree is cut and the latex oozes into a cup fixed by the rubber tapper. The latex is then smoked and vulcanized to make rubber.

Nowadays, much of our rubber is synthetic and is a by-product of oil.

◀ WHERE WAS MAIZE FIRST GROWN?

Maize is an important cereal crop which is now grown in many parts of the world which have hot summers. It is a native of the Americas, and was an important food crop for many Indian tribes before Europeans arrived.

The origin of the modern maize plant (*Zea mays*) is still a mystery. It is an annual plant which now depends on humans for planting. It may be related to *Thea sinte*, a grass which grows in Mexico and whose cobs look very like miniature corn cobs. This plant can reproduce in the wild.

It is possible to cross *Thea sinte* with maize to develop fatter cobs. These look very like corn cobs found by archaeologists in New Mexico which may be 2,000 years old.

For the early European settlers in America, "Indian corn" was often a life-saver. Most American maize is now used as cattle food, but some is eaten as sweet corn or turned into cornflakes or flour.

Zea mays

Thea sinte

◀ WHERE DOES COCOA COME FROM?

Cocoa is made from the beans which develop in the large pod of the cacao tree. Cocoa was drunk by the Aztecs of Central America before Europeans arrived. The cacao tree is still grown in hot, wet areas of Central and South America, but most of the world's cocoa now comes from West Africa.

The tropical cacao tree grows in hot, wet, forested areas near the equator. Large pods, 6 to 13 inches long, grow directly out of its branches and trunk. Each pod contains 30 to 40 beans. The beans are fermented and dried, and then exported for processing into cocoa and chocolate.

The Spanish *conquistadores* liked the bitter cocoa drink they found in Central America, and by the 17th century other Europeans had developed a taste for cocoa. It was the British and French who introduced cacao trees to West Africa, which is now the world's principal cocoa-producing region.

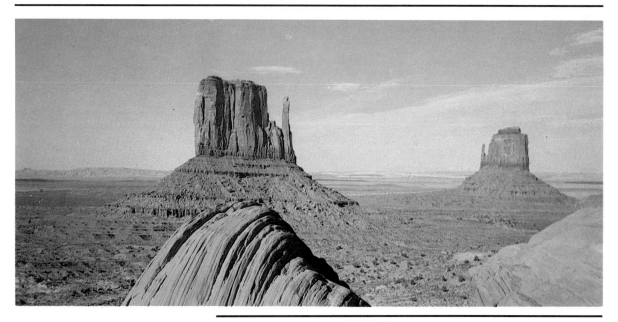

▲ WHERE IS MONUMENT VALLEY?

Monument Valley is part of the Colorado Plateau, in the southwestern United States. The towers, columns and castle-like masses of rock are completely natural monuments.

The rocks of Monument Valley are mainly sandstones with some other sedimentary rocks. These rocks were pushed into an upfold or anticline. As this happened, the layers were stretched and weakened. Faults developed at the edges of the area. Lakes filled the faulted area, and rivers flowed along weaknesses in the rocks. As the rocks were uplifted, the river deepened their valleys.

Over millions of years, many of the rocks eventually eroded away. More resistant rocks have been left standing as columns and as islands of rock called "buttes." The toppled remains of columns litter the floor. Today, the climate is desert and the area is dry, but wind and flash floods continue to erode the area.

▼ WHERE IS THERE SNOW NEAR THE EQUATOR?

Snow lies on the ground all year in places where the temperature is low enough to prevent it from melting completely. Although it is hot at sea level at the equator, it can get very cold indeed at the top of high mountains. Some equatorial mountains are high enough to have permanent snow and ice, such as Mount Kilimanjaro in East Africa and the peaks of the Andes in Ecuador.

Mount Kilimanjaro is a volcano rising high above the East African plains on the borders of Kenya and Tanzania. The highest point is 19,337 feet above sea level.

The place where permanent snow begins is called the snowline. The height of the snowline depends on the temperature and the amount of snow falling. Near the Poles, the snowline is at ground level. At latitude 40° the snowline is at 8,200-16,400 feet, depending on the dryness of the climate. At the equator it is a little over 16,400 feet.

▲ WHERE IS THE GIANT'S CAUSEWAY?

The Giant's Causeway is on the north coast of Northern Ireland. It is a wavecut platform backed by high basalt cliffs. This once-molten rock formed a mass of columns as it cooled. According to Celtic legend, the giant Finn MacCool (or Fingal) built the causeway to link Ireland to Scotland. Similar basalt formations are found in Scotland such as the Isle of Staffa where the sea carved Fingal's Cave.

Sixty million years ago a series of basalt lava flows began to cover large areas of northern Ireland and western Scotland. The lava cooled quickly, forming a dark rock. As it cooled and shrank, joints formed in a fairly regular pattern, giving rise to a vast number of hexagonal columns.

Most of the columns are vertical and form spectacular cliffs over 525 feet high. On the beach the columns have been eroded by the sea. They form amazing steps and pavements, projecting out into the sea toward Scotland.

▼ WHERE IS WAVE ROCK?

Wave Rock is in Western Australia, about 186 miles inland from Perth. It is a great granite rock, 49 feet high, which curves over like an incredible giant wave.

Wave Rock is part of a larger granite area called Hyden Rocks. The nearest settlement is Hyden, a tiny place with fewer than 200 people. Among the nearby granite formations are rocks known locally as Hippo's Yawn, King Rocks and The Humps.

The rock of which Wave Rock is made is about 2,700 million years old. It is one of the rocks which form the ancient base of Australia. Today, the famous formation is colored with vertical streaks which range from deep gray to red, ochre and sandy tints. These colors are the result of staining by various oxides.

The area around Wave Rock is very dry. Visitors can also explore the wildlife reserve around the rock which has many plants and animals native to Australia.

▲ WHERE IS "OLD FAITHFUL"?

"Old Faithful" is one of many geysers and hot springs in Yellowstone National Park in the United States. It got its name because it used to send a jet of steaming water 100 feet up into the air faithfully every 66 minutes. It is not quite so regular today.

Geysers occur when water seeps down through rock layers and is heated up by volcanic activity. The super-heated water is converted into high pressure steam which spurts out of the ground as a geyser.

The whole of Yellowstone National Park is located above a lava-filled hole in the earth's crust. There was once a volcano here, which erupted so violently that the crater was blown apart and the whole area collapsed into the caldera, the remains of the crater.

This part of the USA receives heavy winter snowfalls, so there is a lot of water which is kept simmering on or just below the surface of the earth.

37

PLANTS AND ANIMALS

▶ WHERE AND WHAT ARE BIOMES?

Plants and animals tend to live in communities. Major communities are known as biomes. The world's biomes include coniferous forest, deciduous forest, grassland, desert, tundra and mountains.

Biomes are identified by the types of plant life they contain. The most important factor that determines plant life is climate. Temperature, wind and rainfall work together so that only certain plants can live in a particular area.

At the Poles, temperatures are so low that no plant life can survive. But slightly nearer the equator there is a sparse vegetation known as tundra. This is followed by coniferous forest, of which there is a broad band in the northern hemisphere. Nearer still to the equator, there are areas of deciduous forest. In dry regions this gives way to grassland, and in very dry areas only desert plants can survive. On the other hand there is tropical rain forest in areas that have high rainfall.

Every biome supports its own kinds of animals. But there is another factor that determines the types of animals and plants found in different places. The past and present geography of the world has resulted in many species being restricted to certain regions. For example, lions are found only in Africa.

Caribou

Mountain beaver

Rocky Mountain goat

NORTH AMERICA

Coyote   Bobcat

Pronghorn   Virginia deer

Kangaroo rat   Skunk

TUNDRA

MOUNTAINS

CONIFEROUS FOREST

DECIDUOUS FOREST

TROPICAL FOREST

DESERT

SAVANNAH

TEMPERATE GRASSLAND

MEDITERRANEAN

Peccary

Spider monkey   Anteater

Armadillo

Llama   SOUTH AMERICA

Marmoset

Coypu

▼ **WHY ARE SOME ANIMALS FOUND ONLY IN CERTAIN REGIONS?**

Seas, mountains and deserts form natural barriers to the spread of animals.

The map below shows some of the animals that are confined to particular parts of the world. South America and Australia have unique mammals because these lands were cut off by the sea from the rest of the world during the evolution of the mammals. In other areas, the spread of mammals has been limited by such things as climate, and the presence of deserts and mountain ranges.

EUROPE

Red squirrel

Northern lynx

Brown hare

Roe deer

Saiga antelope

Wild boar

Hedgehog

Dormouse

Jerboa

ASIA

Bactrian camel

Yak

Panda

Mongoose

Tiger

Addax

Fennec

AFRICA

Flying lemur

Giraffe

Lion

Tree shrew

Chimpanzee

Orang-utan

Hippopotamus

Vervet monkey

Golden mole

Kangaroo

Koala

Gemsbok

Dingo

Platypus

AUSTRALIA

▶ WHERE DO PENGUINS BREED?

All penguins live in the Southern Hemisphere. A number of them breed in Antarctic and sub-Antarctic areas.

Penguins spend most of their time at sea, but they all come ashore to breed. Only two, the emperor and Adélie penguins, breed on the Antarctic coast.

Emperor penguins, which are the largest penguins of all, breed in the perpetual darkness of the Antarctic winter. They gather in large "rookeries" on the ice and do not build nests. The males incubate the eggs for two months. Adélie penguins begin nesting in September and October, during the Antarctic spring. They make nests of pebbles on the beaches.

Emperor penguin
Chinstrap penguin   Macaroni penguin   Gentoo penguin

King, macaroni, chinstrap and gentoo penguins breed on sub-Antarctic islands. The king penguin is closely related to the emperor but, like the Adélie, it breeds on stony beaches in the Antarctic spring. The male and female take turns at incubating the egg.

The remaining 11 species all breed farther north. Some, such as the rockhopper penguin, breed on Southern Ocean islands. Others are found on continental coasts.

▶ WHICH SEALS LIVE IN THE ANTARCTIC?

Only four true seals breed in Antarctic waters. They are the crabeater seal, the Weddell seal, the Ross seal and the leopard seal.

Each species of Antarctic seal has its own specialized way of life. Crabeater seals live along the coasts and feed on krill, which they filter from the water using specially adapted teeth.

Ross seals, the smallest of the Antarctic seals, are usually seen on the pack ice and seem to be strong, agile swimmers. They eat squid, fish and krill. Ross seals have been known to play with killer whales, their natural enemies, while feeding on squid.

Weddell seals live along the coasts and are the most placid of the Antarctic seals. They

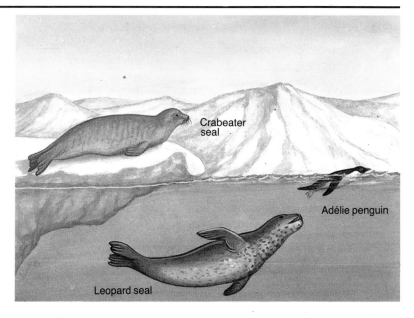
Crabeater seal
Adélie penguin
Leopard seal

feed on fish such as Antarctic cod and icefish, and are known for their diving skills. They can dive down to over 980 feet and stay submerged for over 40 minutes. Their blood and circulatory system are specially adapted for this. Ice covers their feeding areas in winter.

Weddell seals make holes in the ice so that they can come up for air.

Leopard seals are the most carnivorous of the Antarctic seals. They live along the edge of the pack ice and feed on fish, penguins and even the cubs of other seals.

▲ WHERE ARE POLAR BEARS FOUND?

Polar bears live in the snowy wastes of the Arctic. They roam for many miles hunting seals and other animals.

Polar bears are found farther north than any other land mammal. In winter they range across the pack ice of the Arctic Ocean. There they hunt seals, particularly ringed seals, which they capture with great skill. They also eat young walruses and stranded whales.

In spring and summer, polar bears are carried south by the ice. In the tundra they eat plant material such as lichen, moss, grass and berries. Polar bears are good swimmers, although they usually avoid large stretches of open water. They walk with ease across the ice floes because their feet have hairy, non-slip soles.

Polar bears mate in the spring and the cubs are born in December or January. The female gives birth inside a "maternity den" dug into a bank of snow.

▲ WHICH BIRDS NEST IN THE ARCTIC?

Over 100 types of bird nest in the Arctic in summer. Only a few remain during winter.

The Arctic summer lasts only about three months. But during this time many birds nest and rear their young.

Among the summer visitors are ducks, such as long-tailed ducks, geese, such as Brent geese, and swans. They all come to feed on the rich summer vegetation of the tundra wetlands. Insect larvae attract wading birds such as phalaropes, turnstones, knots and dunlins. Flying insects attract warblers, wheatears, fieldfares and yellowhammers. Arctic terns and skuas feed on fish.

As summer ends, many birds fly south to avoid the harsh Arctic winter. Of those that remain, the rock ptarmigan molts its brown feathers and becomes totally white. It shelters in burrows tunneled into the snow. Other birds that spend winter in the Arctic include the snowy owl, raven, gyr falcon, peregrine falcon and the redpoll.

▲ WHERE DO CARIBOU LIVE?

The caribou of North America, together with a number of other mammals, range across the tundra wastes. Reindeer are a semi-domesticated variety of caribou found in northern Europe and Asia.

Caribou and musk oxen are the large herbivores (plant-eaters) of the tundra. In summer they range across the tundra, feeding on many kinds of plants. Their main enemies are wolves and sometimes grizzly bears. Smaller carnivores (flesh-eaters) include foxes and weasels. These hunt shrews, lemmings, ground squirrels and the Arctic hare.

In winter, caribou move south and feed on reindeer moss (a type of lichen), and the twigs of trees such as birch and aspen. Musk oxen remain farther north. In the coldest weather they huddle together to keep warm.

Small mammals tunnel beneath the snow. There they are protected from the biting winds. They feed on seeds and dry grass.

41

▼ WHERE ARE BIGHORN SHEEP FOUND?

Bighorn sheep are found in the Rocky Mountains. They, and the Rocky Mountain goats which also inhabit this region, are agile climbers.

North America has three main mountain ranges. In the east the Appalachians stretch from Labrador to Georgia. In the west there are the coastal ranges that form the Pacific Rim, and the Rocky Mountains which stretch from Alaska to Mexico.

Many animals live in these mountains. Bighorn sheep are sure-footed and scramble among the rocks with ease. Rocky Mountain goats are an American form of goat-antelope. In addition to these animals, there are mountain lions (cougars), Canadian lynxes, beavers, the hoary marmot and the jack rabbit, and many small rodents. Mule deer are found on the lower slopes.

There are also vultures such as the red-headed turkey vulture, and birds of prey such as the golden eagle, bald eagle and osprey.

Mountain lion

Red-headed turkey vulture

Bighorn sheep

▼ WHERE DO IBEXES LIVE?

Ibexes are wild goats. The seven types of ibex are all found in the mountains of Europe, Asia and North Africa. The European species are the Spanish ibex and the Alpine ibex.

The three mountain ranges of Europe – the Carpathians, Alps and Pyrenees – are all relics of the last Ice Age. When the glaciers retreated, these mountains were left as cold "islands" in a much warmer Europe.

Ring ouzel

Golden eagle

Ibex

Marmot

Ibexes are excellent climbers. They sometimes use their dew claws (at the back of each foot) to give them extra grip. Two other cloven-hooved mountain animals are the mouflon (a wild sheep) and the chamois (a goat antelope).

Other alpine animals include lynxes, marmots and susliks (European ground squirrels). The Pyrenees are home to the Pyrenean desman, a water-living relative of the mole. Alpine birds include the alpine chough, ring ouzel, wallcreeper and birds of prey such as the golden eagle.

▼ WHERE DOES THE YAK LIVE?

The yak is the largest of the Himalayan mammals. Wild herds live on the high plateaus of Tibet. Domesticated yak are found all over the highlands of Central Asia.

The Himalayas are home to a number of unique animals. As well as the yak there are several hooved animals such as the Tibetan wild ass, the tahr, markhor, bharal and the largest of all living sheep, the argali. The Siberian ibex is the main prey of the beautiful and rare snow leopard. Smaller animals include the alpine marmot and the high-mountain vole. The large-eared pika is unusual because it does not hibernate during the winter. Instead it lives in its burrow, feeding on hay and other dried plants gathered during the summer.

Himalayan birds include choughs, ravens and the Himalayan snow partridge. Carrion eaters such as the lammergeier vulture, Himalayan griffon and black vulture, are common.

Lammergeier vulture

Snow leopard

Markhor

Yak

▼ WHERE DO PANDAS LIVE?

East of the Himalayas lies Szechwan, in the highlands of southwest China. High in these mountains are the bamboo thickets in which pandas live.

The valleys of Szechwan contain subtropical habitats. These change to broadleaved woodland, coniferous woodland and alpine habitats toward the snow-capped peaks of the mountains. Between 5,900 and 8,200 feet above sea level, the coniferous forest is broken by thickets of bamboo and rhododendron. Here the giant panda lives. It feeds on bamboo shoots and other plants, and even eats small animals occasionally.

The red, or lesser, panda is also found in this region. It too feeds on leaves and fruit, but it is not closely related to the giant panda.

Szechwan is the home of three goat antelopes – the takin, goral and serow. There are also primitive shrews such as the mole shrew, the web-footed water shrew and the Himalayan water shrew.

Giant panda

Lesser panda

▼ WHERE DO LLAMAS LIVE?

The llama is the domesticated pack animal of the High Andes in South America. Its close relatives are the alpaca, guanaco and vicuna.

The Indians of the High Andes domesticated the llama over 4,000 years ago. The llama and the alpaca are thought to have been bred from the guanaco. Vicunas and guanacos have never been domesticated. All these animals are well-adapted for life where the air is thin.

Torrent duck

Spectacled bear

Llama

They have large lungs and extra red blood cells.

The northern part of the Andes has high plains. These are home to many animals, including the spectacled bear, South American mountain tapir, and deer such as the Ecuadorian pudu and the Andean deer, or guemel.

Many birds also inhabit the High Andes. The Andean condor soars high among the peaks. The sierra finch builds its nest among the spiny leaves of puya plants, and torrent ducks live in the tumbling streams.

▼ WHERE ARE THE STRANGEST MOUNTAIN PLANTS FOUND?

Some mountainous regions have very unusual plants. In the mountains of Africa there are giant lobelias and tree groundsels. The Andes have giant lupins and bromeliads. The Chilean pine, or monkey puzzle tree, is one of the few remaining southern conifers.

Mountain plants must survive extreme cold. They are usually low-growing, creeping or cushion-forming plants. However, the giant plants of Africa and South America are extraordinary exceptions.

Giant lobelias and tree groundsels grow to about 19 feet in height. Their leaves are arranged so that they close up at night into "buds." The undersides of the leaves also have a covering of thick, felty hair to protect the buds from the cold.

The giant plants of the Andes are similar. One of the most spectacular is the giant puya, *Puya raymondii*. This has a palm-like trunk, a rosette of long leaves and a tall spike of bird-pollinated flowers.

Monkey puzzle tree

Giant lupin

Giant groundsel

43

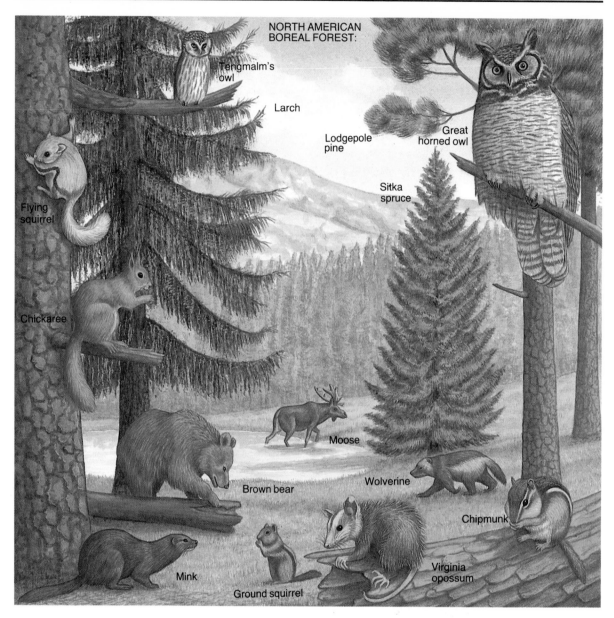

NORTH AMERICAN BOREAL FOREST:

Tengmalm's owl

Larch

Lodgepole pine

Sitka spruce

Great horned owl

Flying squirrel

Chickaree

Moose

Wolverine

Brown bear

Chipmunk

Mink

Ground squirrel

Virginia opossum

▲ WHERE DO MOST CONIFERS GROW?

Below the tundra of the northern hemisphere there is a broad band of poor soils left behind after the last Ice Age. In these cold regions the land is mostly covered with coniferous forest.

The habitat provided by the world's northern coniferous forests is known as taiga. The North American boreal (northern) forest, which is shown above, contains trees such as white and black spruce, sitka spruce, lodgepole pine and tamarack (a larch). In wet areas a few deciduous trees, such as aspen, willow and birch, are found.

In the coniferous forest of northern Europe, the main trees are Norway spruce and Scotch pine. But farther east in the Siberian taiga (shown on the opposite page) the forest becomes more varied. Here the most commonly found conifers include Siberian fir, Siberian larch, stone pine and Siberian spruce. Forest fires are common, so many areas of the Eurasian taiga are at different stages of growth. In the newly burned areas birches and aspens are the most common tree. The Eurasian taiga is the world's largest forest. It is about one-third larger than the entire United States.

Few herbaceous (non-woody) plants grow in the taiga because it is too cold and too dark (the conifers shut out much of the light). Also, the decomposing conifer needles produce a very acid humus. Many kinds of fungi help break down the humus, and some plants do survive in clearings.

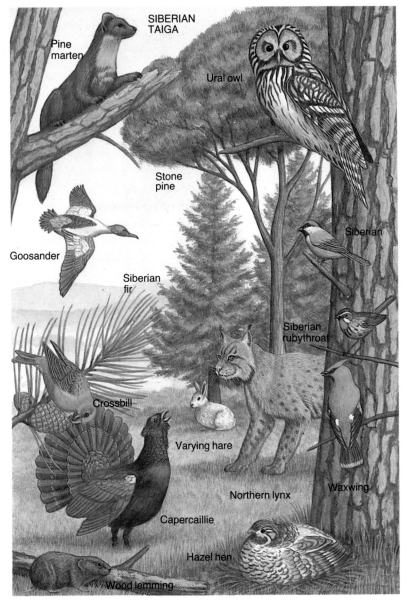

Pine marten
SIBERIAN TAIGA
Ural owl
Stone pine
Goosander
Siberian fir
Siberian
Crossbill
Varying hare
Siberian rubythroat
Northern lynx
Waxwing
Capercaillie
Hazel hen
Wood lemming

◄ WHICH BIRDS LIVE IN CONIFEROUS FORESTS?

The northern forests provide food for many seed-eating and insect-eating birds. Hawks and owls hunt small birds and mammals.

During the summer vast swarms of aphids, mosquitoes and other insects appear in the taiga and provide food for migrant birds such as warblers. Resident insect-eaters include woodpeckers and tits.

Seed-eating birds are also very common. These include the crossbill, the Siberian jay and the pine grosbeak. Waxwings feed on berries as well as seeds. Members of the grouse family, such as the capercaillie, hazel hen and spruce grouse (in North America), feed on seeds, leaves, buds and berries.

Predatory birds include the great horned owl of North America and the Ural owl of Siberia, and a few hawks such as the goshawk. Two unusual taiga birds are the goldeneye and goosander ducks, which nest in abandoned woodpecker holes in trees.

▲ WHICH MAMMALS LIVE IN CONIFEROUS FORESTS?

The coniferous forests of North America and Eurasia support both herbivores and carnivores. The herbivores feed on the leaves, seeds and bark of the trees, and they are hunted by the carnivores. Similar but different species have evolved in each region.

The largest herbivore of the North American forest is the moose (known as the elk in Eurasia) which feeds on low-growing plants and the leaves of deciduous trees. Caribou also venture into the forest during the winter.

Seed-eating mammals include ground squirrels, tree squirrels (such as the gray squirrel), the golden chipmunk, the spruce mouse and the Virginia opossum. Flying squirrels and the chickaree (an American red squirrel) feed on pine cones and toadstools as well as on the eggs and nestlings of small birds. North American tree-porcupines feed on catkins and leaves. In winter they strip the bark off trees and can cause a lot of damage.

The carnivores of the North American forest include the wolf, brown bear, black bear, American mink and wolverine.

Similar animals are found in the Siberian taiga. Here we find the elk, the brown bear, the Siberian chipmunk, the wood lemming, the Siberian weasel, the sable and the pine marten. There are also flying squirrels, ground squirrels and tree squirrels such as the European red squirrel. The northern lynx eats hares, and the wolverine eats northern red-backed voles.

▶ WHY IS DECIDUOUS WOODLAND SO RICH IN WILDLIFE?

Deciduous forests contain a fine undergrowth of small trees, shrubs and herbaceous (non-woody) plants. Such a variety of plants provides food for many animals.

Deciduous forest once covered the entire northern temperate region. Today, in this region, there are only three principal areas of deciduous woodland. The most varied woodland is found in eastern Asia, which has magnolias, tulip trees, sweet gums, planes, horse chestnuts, oaks, beeches, hickories and hornbeams, to name just a few. Many of these trees also grow in the woodlands of eastern North America, although fewer species are found there. European woodlands contain only about 20 species. The main types include oak, ash, beech, hornbeam, field maple, birch and alder.

Deciduous woodland consists of several layers of vegetation. The top layer is formed by tall trees; then come smaller trees and a layer of shrubs such as holly, honeysuckle, blackthorn, elder and hazel. Below this there is a layer of herbaceous plants such as bluebell, primrose and dog's mercury. Finally there is a ground layer, consisting of mosses and other small plants.

The leaves of all these plants are much less tough than the needles of conifers, so they attract a large number of plant-eating animals. The wealth of seeds and fruits also attracts plant-eaters. In turn, many predatory animals feed on the plant-eaters.

▶ WHICH ANIMALS LIVE IN DECIDUOUS FORESTS?

Plant-eating woodland animals range from large species such as deer to small ones such as mice and voles. Predators include foxes and weasels.

Large European herbivores include the red deer, roe deer, fallow deer and wild boar. In North America the white-tailed deer, which was once almost wiped out by hunters, is now increasing in numbers.

Smaller European plant-eaters include the red squirrel, the dormouse, bank vole, wood mouse, hedgehog and rabbit. In America there are similar animals, such as the gray squirrel, eastern chipmunk, white-footed mouse and the pine vole.

The largest predators, such as the wolf, the lynx (in Europe) and the mountain lion (in North America), have almost completely disappeared from deciduous woodland. Instead, today's main predators are foxes such as the European red fox and the North American red and gray foxes. In America other predators include the bobcat, the raccoon, the ring-tailed cat, the skunk, the long-tailed weasel and the short-tailed shrew. European predators include the weasel, stoat, beech marten, polecat and pine marten. Badgers feed on plant material, as well as small animals.

Invertebrate animals play a vital part in the life of deciduous woodland. Worms, beetles and ants help to break down the leaf litter into humus. Many insects are eaten by birds.

▶ WHICH BIRDS LIVE IN DECIDUOUS FORESTS?

Enormous numbers of birds nest and feed in the world's deciduous forests. They feed on insects, seeds, berries, buds and leaves. Birds of prey feed on small birds and mammals.

A number of birds live throughout the year in European deciduous woodland. Omnivorous species include the blackbird, which feeds on insects, worms and berries; the song thrush, which enjoys snails; and the jay, which eats eggs and nestlings and sometimes mice and lizards. The chaffinch feeds on small seeds and insects, as do the wren and the goldfinch. The hawfinch feeds on fruit stones and large seeds. Tits, such as the great tit and blue tit, feed mainly on insects but also eat berries and seeds. Woodpeckers search for insects under pieces of loose bark, and tree creepers dig insects out of small crevices. The wood pigeon feeds on leaves, buds and seeds.

Summer visitors include the nightingale, which feeds mainly on ground insects. The nightjar catches flying insects with its wide-open mouth. Other summer visitors include flycatchers, warblers and the turtle dove.

Woodland birds of prey include the sparrow hawk, kite and buzzard. Tawny owls hunt by night.

American woodland contains a similar range of birds. It includes several woodpeckers and the striking blue jay. Summer visitors include a number of warblers, vireos and tanagers.

EUROPEAN DECIDUOUS WOODLAND

Tawny owl

Sparrowhawk

Greater spotted woodpecker

Blue tit

Jay

Green woodpecker

Lacewing

Gall wasp

Fallow deer

Red fox

Roe deer

Wild boar

Tortoise moth

Stoat

Hedgehog

Badger

Rabbit

Dormouse

NORTH AMERICAN DECIDUOUS WOODLAND

Bobcat

Scarlet tanager

Red-headed woodpecker

Blue jay

White-tailed deer

Gray squirrel

Gray fox

Raccoon

Red-eyed vireo

Skunk

Eastern chipmunk

▼ WHERE DO COYOTES LIVE?

The North American prairies lie between the Mississippi River and the Rocky Mountains. They are the home of a number of plant-eating animals. The coyote is one of the main predators.

The gray wolf was once common on the North American prairies, but it has largely been replaced by the smaller and highly successful coyote, or prairie wolf. The coyote's prey includes jack rabbits, cottontails, prairie dogs and other rodents. It also eats carrion (the carcasses of dead animals).

Coyotes are well-known for their "singing." In the evening two or three coyotes may "sing" together – an eerie sound that has given rise to many legends.

Other predators include the mountain lion, the black-footed ferret and the American badger. The favorite food of the American badger is the prairie dog. American badgers can burrow underground with amazing speed. Unlike European badgers, they hunt by day as well as by night.

▼ WHERE DO PRAIRIE DOGS MAKE THEIR HOMES?

Prairie dogs are so called because of their short barking calls. They dig underground burrows in large colonies on the North American prairies. Prairie dogs are rodents belonging to the squirrel family.

Prairie dogs' colonies, or "towns," can be very large. In 1901 one colony was estimated to cover an area 160 by 380 kilometers. It is thought to have contained about 400 million animals. Today, however, prairie-dog towns are much smaller.

Each town is divided into a number of wards. These, in turn, are divided into coteries, which form the basic family unit. Members of the same coterie groom each other and feed together, and chase off outsiders.

Prairie dogs feed on grasses and other small, fast-growing plants. They have many predators, but an alarm call from one prairie dog is enough to send all those within earshot running for their burrows. It is usually only the sick, slow or unwary that get caught.

▼ WHAT HAPPENED TO THE BISON?

Large herds of bison and pronghorns once roamed the North American prairies. But during the 1800s hunters almost wiped them out.

The American bison is descended from the Asian bison (now extinct) which crossed into America via the Bering land bridge that existed a million years ago. At one time there were probably about 50 million plains bison in North America, but by 1889 there were only 540 left. The rest had been slaughtered for their meat, bones or hides – and often simply for sport. However, since the bison became a protected animal, numbers have increased and there are now several thousand in national parks.

The story of the pronghorn is a similar one. About 20 million years ago, there were probably over 40 million of these animals. In the 1800s, European settlers hunted them in great numbers and by 1925 there were only about 30,000 pronghorns left. But they have now grown in number to about 400,000.

▼ WHERE DOES THE VISCACHA LIVE?

The South American pampas is the home of some unique animals. These include armadillos and the viscacha, mara and aperea.

The temperate grassland known as the pampas is found on the plains of Argentina and Uruguay. Here it is possible to travel hundreds of miles without seeing a tree.

There are few large herbivores. The rare pampas deer is the largest, and there are occasional herds of guanaco.

Small herbivores include a number of South America's unique range of rodents. Viscachas tunnel labyrinth-like towns underground. The mara, or Patagonian hare, digs deep burrows. This animal is also found farther south on the dry Patagonian steppe, and manages to live without drinking. Other grassland rodents include the pampas guinea pig, or aperea, and the tuco-tuco. The aperea does not burrow. Instead it hides in tufts of grass.

Several armadillos are found in the pampas. They include the nine-banded, giant, hairy, and fairy armadillos. The giant anteater also roams the plains.

Pampas predators include the southern gray fox, the long-legged maned wolf and the rare pampas cat.

Pampas birds include the rhea, the rufous ovenbird and the burrowing owl, which is also found in the dry areas of North America. There are also some species of tinamou. These are shy, partridge-like birds that can fly, but rarely take to the air.

◄ WHY DO SO FEW TREES GROW ON GRASSLAND?

Grassland occurs in those parts of the world where the rainfall is low or very seasonal. Fires and grazing animals help to prevent trees from growing.

Some temperate parts of the world, especially the centers of large continents, receive most of their rain at particular times of the year. In summer such areas have dry, hot weather and in winter there is often a thick covering of snow.

Trees find it difficult to grow in these conditions and so the land is mainly covered with grasses mixed with small herbaceous plants. Fires are common during the dry season and these help to keep down the trees. Grazing animals also help to maintain temperate grassland, as they nibble off the young shoots of any trees before they can grow.

Temperate grasslands include the steppes of central Asia, the North American prairies, the South American pampas and the South African veld.

Guanaco

Rhea

Maned wolf

Pampas deer

Mara

Hairy armadillo

Rufous ovenbird

Cavy

Viscacha

▶ WHAT IS SAVANNAH?

Savannah is tropical grassland. It occurs in hot regions where rainfall is very seasonal. The best-known savannah is that of Africa.

The African savannah is a dry, dusty region for most of the year, and the rainy season lasts for only four months. The most common grass is red oat grass, and the savannah is also dotted with acacia and baobab trees. Some areas are fairly well wooded.

▶ WHICH BIRDS LIVE IN THE SAVANNAH?

The African savannah supports huge numbers of insect-eating and seed-eating birds. Among the most notable of African birds is the ostrich.

The huge, flightless ostrich is the world's largest living bird. It feeds on fruit, seeds and small animals. The savannah is also the home of the world's heaviest flying bird, the kori bustard, which may weigh over 110 pounds. Bustards also feed on both plant material and animals.

Oxpeckers are common on the savannah. They perch on the backs of grazing animals, and feed on ticks and other parasites. Other savannah birds include bulbuls, shrikes, marabou storks, cranes and ground hornbills. Weaver-birds build elaborate hanging nests in trees, as do their close relatives, the queleas. Huge flocks of queleas can cause a lot of damage to trees.

Birds of prey include the secretary bird and lanner falcon. Several types of vulture feed on the carcasses of dead animals.

Elephants

Giraffe

Gerenuk

Zebras

Cheetah

Thomson's gazelle

Jackal

Griffon vulture

White-headed vulture

▲ WHICH SAVANNAH ANIMALS LIVE IN HERDS?

The savannah is populated with large, sometimes vast, herds of grazing hooved mammals. Zebras and wildebeests form some of the largest herds.

A lone antelope grazing on the savannah is open to attack. The chances of such an animal surviving are small. On the other hand, the members of a herd give each other some protection. They can warn each other of the presence of danger. An individual animal within a herd also stands a much greater chance of not being singled out by a predator. When a predator does attack, the milling, rushing herd may confuse it.

The most abundant hooved mammals are wildebeests, zebras, hartebeests and Thomson's gazelles. They normally live in small scattered herds, but during the calving season they gather together in larger herds for protection. At the start of the dry season they also migrate in vast herds to moister areas.

50

Weaver birds

Wildebeest

White rhino

Ostriches

Oxpecker

Grant's gazelle

Lion

◀ HOW DO SO MANY
ANIMALS LIVE TOGETHER IN
THE SAVANNAH?

If all the savannah plant-eaters grazed in the same way, they would soon run out of food. But in fact each species feeds in a different way. In some cases the feeding method of one species actually helps another.

The herbivores of the savannah do not compete with each other for food. On the grassy plains of the Serengeti National Park, zebras chew off the coarse tops of grasses before moving on to another area. They are followed by wildebeests and topis, which eat the leafy centers of the plants almost down to the ground. Finally, Thomson's gazelles eat fallen seeds and young shoots at ground level. The gazelles benefit from the feeding of the earlier, larger animals. They can find their food easily because the tall grasses have been trampled and eaten.

In more wooded areas of savannah, competition for food is avoided in a similar way. Warthogs graze and also dig for bulbs and tubers on the ground. Springboks feed mainly on grass, but other antelopes are only partial grazers. They feed on the leaves and twigs of bushes and trees as well as on grass, and each species has its own preferred type of food. Dik-diks, steinboks, Grant's gazelles, kudus, elands and white rhinos browse increasingly higher levels of the bushes and trees. The topmost branches are browsed by elephants, which often destroy whole trees, and also by giraffes.

▲ WHICH ARE THE SAVANNAH HUNTERS?

Where there are so many plant-eating animals, there are naturally a number of predators. Each species of predator has its own method of hunting.

The best-known savannah hunter is the lion, the "King of Beasts." Lions often hunt in groups, or prides, and it is the lionesses who usually do the work of stalking and killing the prey.

The world's fastest animal, the cheetah, is also a savannah hunter. It approaches stealthily to within 350 feet or so of its prey and then runs it down by sheer speed. The leopard, on the other hand, prefers to lie in wait in a tree or among any suitable cover. The victim is then taken with a short, powerful charge.

Other savannah predators include the wild dog, serval, bat-eared fox, civet and banded mongoose. Jackals and hyenas hunt small animals. They are also scavengers, often taking over the abandoned kills of larger predators.

▼ WHERE IS THE DESERT COLD IN WINTER?

The deserts of Central Asia are baked dry during the summer. But in winter they are exposed to icy air from the Arctic. Even so, many animals survive there.

The Central Asian deserts stretch from the Caspian Sea eastward to the Gobi Desert in Mongolia. Some of the most common animals are the jerboas, of which there are a number of species. Other rodents include the desert hedgehog and long-eared hedgehog. Large mammals are more common than in other deserts. The Bactrian camel lives in the Gobi Desert. Wild asses and Mongolian gazelles (the most northerly of all gazelles) also roam the deserts of Asia. Snakes and lizards are very common. One of the largest desert snakes is the lebatine viper.

A number of birds can be found in the Asian deserts, particularly in spring, when food is plentiful. They include desert warblers, desert larks, stone curlews, desert shrikes, sandgrouse and hawks.

Eared agama

Jerboa

Grey monitor

Bactrian camel

▼ CAN FISH SURVIVE IN HOT WATER?

At the southern end of Death Valley in Nevada will be found a series of small streams and lakes. These are the home of desert pupfish, which survive water temperatures that would kill most fish.

The streams and lakes these pupfish live in were once very large lakes. During the last Ice Age they covered much of what is now desert. Pupfish feed on the algae that grow in these warm waters. They can survive temperatures of just over 42°C.

The populations of the various species of pupfish were once numbered in tens of thousands. Today, however, predators and irrigation projects have reduced their numbers.

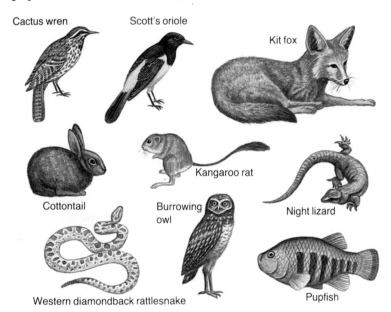

Cactus wren

Scott's oriole

Kit fox

Cottontail

Kangaroo rat

Burrowing owl

Night lizard

Pupfish

Western diamondback rattlesnake

▲ WHERE DO CACTI GROW?

Cacti are the most familiar of all desert plants. But they are not found in all deserts – only in those of North and South America. They help support a number of desert animals.

Pronghorns sometimes visit the desert to feed on cacti and shrubs, but most North American desert animals are much smaller. The kangaroo rat is a jumping rodent that burrows into the sandy ground and shelters in its burrow during the day. At night it comes out to feed on seeds and other plant material. It probably never drinks. Other small herbivores include the desert cottontail, wood rat and grasshopper mouse. Desert hunters include the bobcat and the kit fox which resembles the Saharan fennec.

Among the many snakes and lizards are the American sidewinder, a rattlesnake, and the Gila monster, one of the world's two poisonous lizards. Insect-eating birds include Scott's oriole, the cactus wren and the whippoorwill, which hibernates during the winter. Elf owls nest in abandoned woodpecker holes in saguaro cactus stems. The burrowing owl shares the underground homes of other animals, including, on occasions, rattlesnakes!

▼ WHICH IS THE WORLD'S LARGEST DESERT?

The world's largest desert is the Sahara Desert, which forms a broad band across North Africa. In most places the annual rainfall is less than 4 inches and it is one of the hottest places in the world.

Desert is often thought of as stretches of rolling sand dunes. But, although the Sahara does contain seas of dunes (known as ergs), there are other types of desert as well. There are raised plateaus of rock known as hamadas, and large flat, stony regions known as regs.

Despite this bleak landscape, the Sahara is far from lifeless. Tough, hardy plants provide food for many insects such as beetles, grasshoppers and crickets. Even moths and butterflies appear after the occasional rainstorm. In turn, these insects are eaten by other animals such as lizards, snakes, scorpions, jerboas, gerbils, sand rats and desert hedgehogs. Larger animals include the fennec, which preys on small rodents, and the addax, a desert antelope. Desert birds include sand grouse, larks and several species that fly in to feed on seeds and insects.

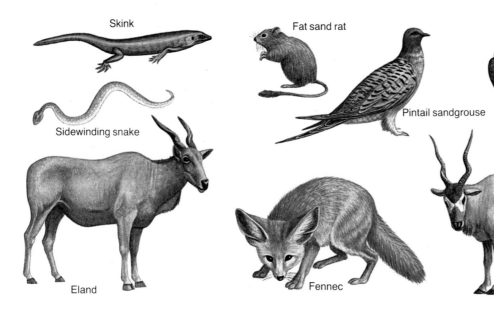

Skink

Fat sand rat

Lanner falcon

Sidewinding snake

Pintail sandgrouse

Eland

Fennec

Addax

▲ HOW DO DESERT ANIMALS SURVIVE?

The desert presents its inhabitants with several problems. The biggest of these are how to stay cool and how to get enough moisture. Desert animals have evolved a number of adaptations that enable them to survive.

Many desert animals have large ears, feet and tails. These are used as radiators to help get rid of excess heat. Large ears have an additional advantage. They enable their owners to hear the slightest sound in the still desert air. The hearing of the fennec, for example, is particularly keen.

Most desert animals shelter from the heat of the sun during the day and are active only at night or in the early morning and evening. But some animals are out and about during the day. A desert locust keeps cool by turning its head toward the sun, thus exposing the least possible area of its body to the searing heat.

Because water is scarce in the desert, animals have to make full use of the little they can get. Many desert animals do not sweat and they produce very concentrated urine and dry feces. Large herbivores, which cannot shelter in burrows, have the greatest problem. The eland, which lives near the edge of the Sahara, manages to find some shelter and some water. But the addax and the oryx survive in the hottest areas without drinking. All their water is obtained from dew and the sparse plant-life. Few birds nest in the desert, though the sand grouse is an exception. It flies long distances to find water, which it carries back to its nestlings by soaking its breast feathers.

Movement in sandy areas of desert is not easy. Many desert rodents are jumping rather than walking animals. The horned viper of the Sahara sidewinds across the sand and sandfish (types of skink) almost "swim."

53

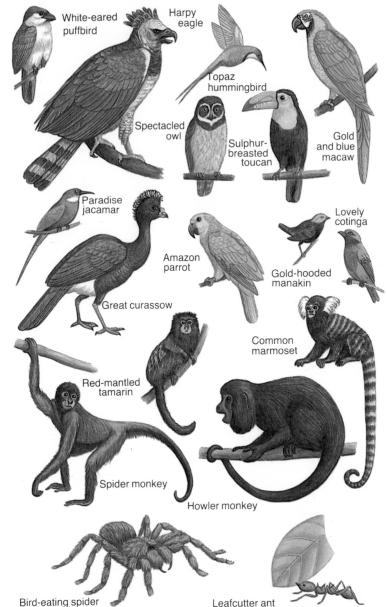

White-eared puffbird

Harpy eagle

Topaz hummingbird

Spectacled owl

Sulphur-breasted toucan

Gold and blue macaw

Paradise jacamar

Lovely cotinga

Amazon parrot

Gold-hooded manakin

Great curassow

Common marmoset

Red-mantled tamarin

Spider monkey

Howler monkey

Bird-eating spider

Leafcutter ant

▶ WHERE IS THE WORLD'S LARGEST RAIN FOREST?

Tropical rain forests occur in warm, moist regions near the equator. The largest area of rain forest is the Amazon basin in South America.

Of all the world's biomes, tropical rain forests contain the greatest variety of wildlife. This is because these areas receive an enormous amount of warmth, sunlight and rain. In the wettest areas plant growth, flowering and fruiting continues throughout the year. This kind of habitat provides homes and food for ten times the number of animals found in deciduous woodland.

Five layers can be seen in tropical forest. At ground level, fungi, mosses and ferns grow in the rich leaf litter. The second layer consists of tree ferns, shrubs and lianas. Next there is a layer of young tree crowns, and above this is the thick canopy, the crowns of mature trees. The topmost layer consists of the few trees that stand above the canopy.

Tropical rain forests contain a wealth of insect life. There are countless butterflies, beetles, mantises, stick insects and crickets. Many of these have amazing forms of camouflage. Others have bright warning colors or markings that are used to startle predators.

Amphibians and reptiles are also common. In the Amazon forest arrow-poison frogs, tree frogs and horned frogs prey on insects and other small animals. Snakes include the anaconda, boa constrictor and coral snakes. Lizards include the green iguana, anole and tegu.

▲ WHICH KINDS OF BIRD LIVE IN THE RAIN FOREST?

The canopy of any tropical rain forest provides food for a host of birds. Many feed on the nectar, fruits and seeds of the trees.

The brightly colored birds of the Amazon forest blend with the luminous greens, reds and yellows of the flowers and foliage. Toucans, parrots, parakeets, macaws and curassows feed on the plentiful supply of fruit. Smaller fruit-eaters include manakins, cotingas and bellbirds. Insect-eaters include jacamars, puff-birds, trogons and tanagers. Hummingbirds and honeycreepers feed on nectar.

One of the strangest birds of the Amazon is the hoatzin, whose young have claws on their wings to help them scramble about the trees. One of the few birds of prey is the harpy eagle.

A similar range of birds can be found in the African rain forests. As in South America, there are a number of parrots, but in Africa hornbills take the place of toucans.

◄ **WHICH MAMMALS LIVE IN THE AMAZON RAIN FOREST?**

Tropical forests are inhabited by a large number of monkeys. The Amazon forest is also the home of sloths and other climbing mammals.

New World monkeys abound in the Amazon forest. Troops of capuchins, titis, spider monkeys, woolly monkeys, squirrel monkeys, tamarins and marmosets (the smallest of all monkeys) spend their days in the forest canopy, searching for fruit, flowers and buds. Douroucoulis are the only ones that sleep during the day. Uakaris and sakis move around singly or in pairs. The largest of the South American monkeys are the howler monkeys, which set up a howling chorus just after sunrise to establish the whereabouts of rival groups.

Most of these monkeys have grasping, or prehensile, tails. This is also true of other South American forest animals, such as the Brazilian tree-porcupine, the kinkajou and the tamandua, or collared anteater. Other tree dwellers include the sloths. They hang from branches, using their huge claws, and move very slowly through the forest, feeding on leaves. Coatis are excellent climbers and eat almost anything that is edible, as does their relative the crab-eating raccoon.

Rodents, such as acoushis and agoutis, forage on the forest floor, eating all kinds of plant material, especially fallen fruit and nuts. Forest hunters include the jaguar, ocelot, margay cat and tayra, a member of the weasel family.

◄ **WHICH MAMMALS LIVE IN AFRICAN RAIN FORESTS?**

The rain forests of Africa are the home of a number of Old World monkeys and other primates. There are also several forest antelopes.

The largest group of African monkeys are the guenons, such as the Diana monkey, the De Brazza monkey, Hamlyn's monkey and the moustached monkey. Each one of these has its own preferred forest layer. Other African forest monkeys include the colobus monkey and the drill, which is a ground-living baboon.

African forests also contain other primates, such as babies and galagos, the potto and the angwantibo. In addition, there are apes – the chimpanzee and gorilla.

Hoofed mammals are common in African forests. They include the okapi, bongo, water chevrotain, several duikers and giant forest hogs. Small mammals include elephant shrews, squirrels and scalytails. The forest hunters include the leopard, African golden cat, forest genet and slender mongoose.

Colobus monkey

Chimpanzee

Gorilla

Tree pangolin

Royal antelope

Bongo

Genet

Elephant shrew

Water chevrotain

Okapi

▲ WHERE DO FLYING LEMURS LIVE?

Flying lemurs, or colugos, are found in the tropical forests of Southeast Asia. These forests are also inhabited by a number of primates.

The name "flying lemur" is misleading. This animal does not actually fly, and it is no relation of the true lemurs of Madagascar. However, flying lemurs are superb gliders and can glide from tree to tree with amazing accuracy. They have features somewhere between those of bats and insectivores, and are classified in a mammal order by themselves.

Flying lemurs are not the only gliders of these forests. There are also flying squirrels, flying frogs, flying lizards and even gliding snakes.

The Asian forests are the home of the primitive tree shrews and a number of primates. These include the tiny tarsiers and the lorises. The two main groups of monkey are the langurs and the macaques, and there are two kinds of ape – the gibbon and the orangutan.

▲ WHERE DO TIGERS AND RHINOCEROSES LIVE?

Rhinoceroses are found in Africa and Southeast Asia. Tigers are found only in Asia.

Five species of rhinoceros exist today. Two of these, the black rhinoceros and the white rhinoceros, are found in Africa. Both African species have two horns.

The three one-horned species are found in India, Sumatra and Java. They are all in danger of extinction, but the most endangered is the Javan rhinoceros, which survives only in one small reserve.

The tiger is a highly adaptable animal. It originated in the cold northeast region of China. From there it spread northward into the snowy wastes of Siberia, westward to the Caspian Sea and southward into the tropical rain forests of India and Southeast Asia. Today naturalists recognize eight races of tiger. However, they differ only in their markings. Once all the races were widespread, but now they are all endangered.

Silvered langurs

Proboscis monkey

Mudskippers

▲ WHERE IS THE HOME OF THE ORANGUTAN?

The orangutan is found only in the rain forests of Sumatra and Borneo. It was once widespread throughout Southeast Asia, but is now in danger of extinction because the rain forests are being cleared and young orangutans are captured for zoos.

The name *orangutan* means "man of the woods." Like humans, individual orangutans are easy to identify by their facial features and expressions. However, the orangutan is less closely related to humans than the chimpanzee or gorilla.

Like the gibbons, the other Asian apes, orangutans are tree-living animals. They can swing from branch to branch or walk along branches with great ease.

Adult males live alone for most of the time. Their huge throat pouches are used to produce loud booming sounds. Females often travel about in small groups with their young. At night an orangutan sleeps in a rough "nest" in a tree.

▲ WHERE ARE MANGROVE FORESTS FOUND?

Mangrove swamps occur where rain forest borders the sea. Mangrove forests are found in many tropical parts of the world.

Along the coasts and estuaries of tropical rain forests, the rivers deposit a rich, fine silt which forms extensive mudflats in the tidal waters. Trees and shrubs take root in the mud. The most common tree is the mangrove. Many mangroves have stilt-like roots for support. Others have special breathing roots that stick out of the mud and take in oxygen (the mud contains very little oxygen). The tangled plant life of a mangrove swamp helps to bind the mud, and in doing so gradually reclaims new land from the sea.

Mangrove forests are extensive in Southeast Asia. The forests of Borneo are the home of certain langurs, such as the dusky langur, the silver leaf monkey, the strange proboscis monkey and crab-eating macaques.

Little king bird
of paradise

Count Raggi's
bird of paradise

Greater bird of paradise

Red bird
of paradise

Wilson's bird
of paradise

◄ WHERE DO BIRDS OF PARADISE LIVE?

Birds of paradise are some of the world's most colorful and spectacular birds. Most of the 43 species are found in the forests of New Guinea.

The ancestor of the bird of paradise was probably a drab, crow-like bird that made its way to New Guinea from Asia. Today, a few members of the family are still rather drab, but others are startlingly colorful.

As is the case with many birds, it is the male bird of paradise that is the most splendid. Its bright colors and long feathers are used to attract a female mate. Display techniques vary, enabling females to recognize males of their own species easily. Some birds of paradise even display upside down. After mating, the females fly away to build their nests and rear the young on their own.

The feathers of these birds were once much sought by European hat-makers, and thousands of birds were killed each year. Today, however, birds of paradise are protected.

Honey possum pollinating
a Banksia flower

▲ WHERE ARE BANKSIAS FOUND?

The southwestern corner of Australia has a high rainfall and luxuriant vegetation. It is cut off from the rest of Australia by the desert and is the home of some unique plants and animals. Among these are the flowering trees known as Banksias, and their pollinators.

Most brightly colored flowers are pollinated by insects. But Banksia flowers are pollinated by birds such as honeyeaters, which visit the flowers to drink nectar. Small marsupials such as the honey possum also visit these flowers. They use their long tongues to probe deep into the flowers. Pollen sticks to the fur on their faces. This is then carried to other flowers.

Other bird-pollinated plants in this part of Australia include certain eucalyptus trees which are pollinated by parakeets. A nectar-feeding parakeet has a long tongue tipped with a brush-like organ. The "brush" soaks up nectar and picks up pollen as it is withdrawn from the flower.

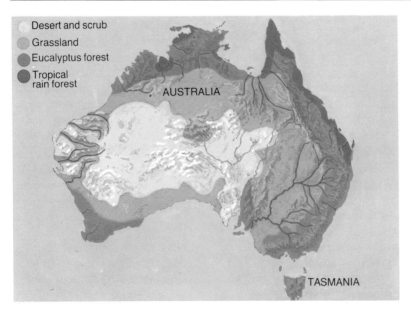

Legend:
- Desert and scrub
- Grassland
- Eucalyptus forest
- Tropical rain forest

AUSTRALIA

TASMANIA

Pretty-faced wallaby

Red kangaroo

Koala

Tiger cat

Wombat

Tasmanian devil

Sugar glider

Tasmanian wolf

▲ WHAT DO MARSUPIALS EAT?

There are very few placental mammals in Australia. Instead, most Australian mammals are marsupials (pouched mammals). They occupy almost all the habitats that would normally be taken by placentals. Marsupials therefore range from peaceful grazers to fierce carnivores.

In the Americas, Europe and Asia, grassland and scrub are grazed by hoofed mammals. There were no such mammals in Australia. Instead, kangaroos and wallabies became the grazers. They range from the large gray kangaroo and red kangaroo to the tiny rat kangaroo. Among this group there are also browsing forest animals, such as the tree kangaroo and the shrub wallaby.

There are no tree-living primates or rodents in Australia. Their habitats are taken by the phalangers and opossums. The cuscus, for example, is a monkey-like phalanger. Other phalangers and opossums resemble squirrels. Flying phalangers, such as the sugar glider, look exactly like flying squirrels. Most of these animals feed on plants but they also eat insects, eggs and even small birds. The koala eats the leaves of certain types of eucalyptus tree.

Rabbits and some small ground rodents have been introduced into Australia. Their marsupial equivalents, the wombat and the bandicoot, are now declining in numbers. Two other Australian ground-dwellers are the marsupial mole, which is almost identical to a placental mole, and the numbat, which is the equivalent of an anteater.

Marsupial carnivores include the dasyures, such as the tiger cat, and the eastern native cat, or quoll. These animals look more like mongooses than cats, but they are agile climbers and they stalk their prey. The so-called marsupial mice are the smallest carnivores. The largest are the Tasmanian wolf, or thylacine, and the Tasmanian devil, which eats carrion as well as live prey. Both these animals now live only in Tasmania, and the thylacine is probably extinct.

Himatione sanguinea

Vestiaria coccinea

Hemignathus procerus

Psittirostra cantans

▲ HOW MANY KINDS OF HAWAIIAN HONEYCREEPER ARE THERE?

On the remote islands of Hawaii honeycreepers have become even more varied than the Galapagos finches. About 23 species evolved, of which 14 still exist today.

The ancestors of the Hawaiian honeycreepers were probably finch-like birds (possibly tanagers) that managed to make the 2,170-mile journey from North America. The honeycreepers which evolved from these travelers vary in size and coloring, but the main differences are in their feeding habits – which are indicated by the shapes of their bills.

Some honeycreepers have long, curved bills and brush-tipped tongues for drinking nectar. Others use their curved bills to probe for insects. Honeycreepers with shorter bills use them as woodpeckers do to chisel away at the bark of trees to get at insects. Seed- and fruit-eating honeycreepers have short, stout bills like those of finches.

▼ WHY ARE ISLAND ANIMALS DIFFERENT FROM OTHERS?

New species evolve in isolated places. Remote islands with stable climates provide ideal places for new species to evolve.

When a new island forms far away from any large continent, it takes time for animals to colonize it. The few animals that do arrive have to adapt to their new surroundings. For those that can adapt there are tremendous advantages.

Unhindered by the animals that formerly preyed on them or competed with them for food, they can take over all the different types of habitat that are so freely available.

This process is called adaptive radiation and it can be seen in the finches of the Galapagos Islands. The ancestors of these finches probably flew in from South America. Over a long period of time they gave rise to the 15 different species that exist today. Each one has evolved to suit a particular type of habitat and method of feeding.

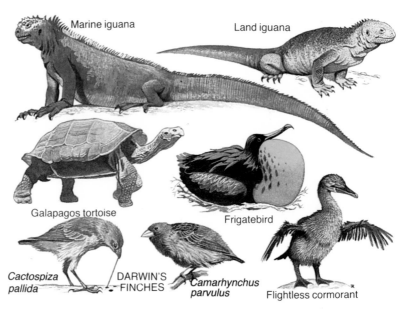

Marine iguana

Land iguana

Galapagos tortoise

Frigatebird

Cactospiza pallida

DARWIN'S FINCHES

Camarhynchus parvulus

Flightless cormorant

▲ WHICH ANIMALS LIVE IN THE GALAPAGOS ISLANDS?

The Galapagos Islands were formed about two million years ago. Since that time several unique species have evolved there. As well as the finches, there are giant tortoises, marine iguanas and flightless cormorants.

A Galapagos giant tortoise can measure over 3 feet in length. At one time each island had its own race of tortoise, but during the 1600s and 1700s visiting sailors killed them for

food, and some races have disappeared completely.

Iguanas probably arrived on floating logs from South America. Water and food are not as easy to find on these islands, and the iguanas adapted in two ways. Today there are land iguanas that feed on fruit and cacti and marine iguanas that feed on seaweed.

The islands provide nesting sites for a number of sea birds. These include a flightless cormorant, the Galapagos penguin, and oceanic sea birds such as frigatebirds and boobies.

▼ WHERE ARE MOST FLIGHTLESS BIRDS FOUND?

Flightless birds tend to live where there are few, if any, predators. A large number of flightless birds are found in Australia and New Zealand.

One of the main advantages of being able to fly is the ability to escape from predators. However, for birds that evolved in places where there were no enemies, this ability became less necessary and many abandoned flight altogether.

Unfortunately, flightless birds are extremely vulnerable to introduced predators such as cats and foxes, and to other animals such as rats, which eat their eggs and compete with them for food. Many flightless birds have also been hunted by people. Some, such as the elephant bird of Madagascar, the moa of New Zealand, many flightless island rails, and the Mauritian dodo, are now extinct.

Several flightless birds do still exist in New Zealand. The three species of kiwi are nocturnal forest dwellers, and this has probably helped them to survive. The weka, one of the few remaining flightless rails, actually thrives on introduced animals: it eats rats and mice! On the other hand, the coot-like takahe (another member of the rail family) is in danger of extinction.

In Australia the common emu still exists in fairly large numbers, but it is the only survivor of several species of emu that lived there before the arrival of humans. Its close relatives, the cassowaries, are secretive forest dwellers.

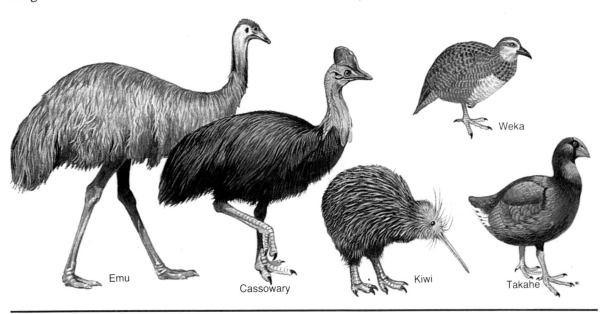

Emu

Cassowary

Weka

Kiwi

Takahe

▶ WHERE DO CRABS CLIMB TREES?

Some island animals are particularly strange and unusual. The robber crabs that live on islands in the Indian and Pacific oceans are adept tree climbers.

Crabs are usually thought of as sea creatures, but robber crabs and other land crabs are well-adapted for living on land. Although the larvae of such crabs live in the sea, an adult robber crab will drown if left in water for more than a day.

Robber crabs are expert at climbing trees. But why they do so is something of a mystery. It was once thought that they climbed coconut palms to dislodge coconuts, which they then cracked open and ate. However, a robber crab is quite unable to get inside a coconut. And, in fact, its main food is carrion: dead animal matter that is washed up on beaches. They do eat the flesh of coconuts, but only after the coconuts have been broken into by other animals. They also eat certain fruits.

Arctic tern

Arctic skua

Red-throated pipit

Wheatear

Arctic warbler

Siberian willow warbler

Swallow

Tiger shrike

Snow goose

Grey whale

Cuckoo

Bobolink

Greater shearwater

Golden plover

Short-tailed shearwater

Equator

■ Feeding area

● Breeding area

Tristan da Cunha

Wandering albatross

Arctic tern

Arctic tern

Wandering albatross

▲ WHY DO BIRDS MIGRATE?

A migrating bird typically moves from a summer breeding area to a winter feeding area. The reasons for such migrations include the availability of food and avoiding extreme cold.

The migrations of northern birds may have started at the end of the last Ice Age. As the ice cap melted, some birds moved north in summer to take advantage of the food that became available. Each winter they retreated south again, but gradually their journeys became longer and longer.

The most northerly birds migrate south to avoid the Arctic winter. The Arctic tern covers the longest distance: it migrates all the way to the Antarctic. Farther south, the migratory birds are mostly insect-eaters that cannot find enough food in winter. Seed-eaters and omnivorous birds often remain in the same area all year.

▲ WHERE DO SHEARWATERS MIGRATE TO?

Shearwaters, or petrels, are sea birds that breed in large colonies in the same place each year. Outside the breeding season some shearwaters make long journeys.

The Manx shearwater breeds only on certain European coasts. But during the remaining months of the year it wanders around the Atlantic Ocean. The greater shearwater breeds on the island of Tristan da Cunha between November and April, but spends July and August in the North Atlantic.

Between October and March, short-tailed shearwaters breed in thousands off the coasts of Tasmania and southeastern Australia. But in April they begin a complete circuit of the Pacific Ocean. This migration enables them to take advantage of the abundant fish supplies of the North Pacific Ocean.

▲ WHY DO WHALES MIGRATE?

Most migratory animals breed in their northern range. But northern whales migrate south to breed in warmer waters. Southern whales migrate in the opposite direction.

The best-known whale migration is that of the California gray whale. This animal feeds all summer in the Bering Sea. Its autumn migration route follows the coast of North America to breeding lagoons off the coast of California.

Other migrating whales include the blue whale and the humpback whale. There are populations of these whales in both the Northern and Southern Hemispheres. The northern populations move south to summer breeding grounds, and the southern populations move north. But because the seasons of the two hemispheres are different, the two populations never meet.

▼ WHERE DO MONARCH BUTTERFLIES MIGRATE TO?

The two main populations of monarch butterflies are found in North and South America. Both populations move nearer to the equator in the fall.

Most butterflies migrate to some extent, but monarchs make longer journeys than most. They may fly 1,800 miles to their winter feeding areas.

In summer the North American population of monarchs is spread across southern Canada and the northern U.S. In autumn they gather in groups and move south until the whole population reaches the southern part of North America. There they spend the winter in huge clusters.

In spring they mate and begin to move north again. But the adults that set out are not those that eventually reach Canada. Two or three generations may pass before the population is once again back in its northern area.

North American Monarch butterfly

▼ WHERE DO GREEN TURTLES LAY THEIR EGGS?

Like all sea turtles, green turtles lay their eggs on land. They spend the rest of their time at sea, but each year they return to the same beaches to lay their eggs.

Green turtles are found in tropical and subtropical waters all round the world. They were once very numerous, but they have been hunted by people for their flesh. Today, there are only about a dozen major nesting beaches left. These beaches are usually on islands. A green turtle may travel as far as 1,200 miles to reach its own nesting beach.

On reaching the beach, a female waits until night. Then she crawls out, digs a nest and lays about 100 eggs which she covers with sand. About eight weeks later the eggs hatch and the young wait near the surface for a few days. Then, during the night, they emerge and head for the sea. Many are eaten by predators such as crabs, cats, sea birds and sharks.

▼ WHERE DO EELS BREED?

Eels live in fresh water and migrate to the sea to lay their eggs. They breed only in the Sargasso Sea.

When female eels are between 7 and 12 years old (4-8 years old in the case of males) they leave their inland rivers and head downstream to the Atlantic Ocean. They spawn in the Sargasso Sea.

The adults die and the larvae hatch out. As they drift away from the Sargasso Sea, they grow. By the time they reach the rivers they have changed into adults.

The European and American eels are usually thought of as being two different species, but in fact there is little difference between them. If they are different species, how do the young larvae sort themselves out as they leave the Sargasso Sea? One idea is that adult eels from Europe do not in fact ever reach the breeding area, and that both the European and American eels come from eggs laid by American eels.

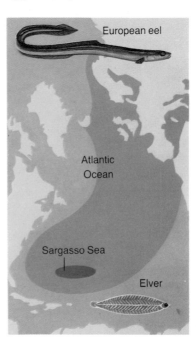

European eel

Atlantic Ocean

Sargasso Sea

Elver

THE PAST

▼ WHERE WERE THE OLDEST HUMAN FOOTPRINTS FOUND?

Almost four million years ago, creatures very like ourselves walked the earth. We know this because they left their footprints behind.

At Olduvai Gorge in Tanzania, East Africa, scientists have unearthed some of the oldest known human remains. They found bones, stone tools, and even signs of a crude stone shelter.

At nearby Laetoli, an even more amazing find was three sets of footprints, preserved in a layer of volcanic ash. They show that three people (two adults and a child) passed that way about 3,700,000 years ago. The footprints provide one of the earliest clues to the puzzle of when the first true humans appeared on earth.

▼ WHERE DID FARMERS FIRST GROW CROPS?

We do not know exactly where people first discovered how to grow plants for food. It was somewhere in the Middle East, about 9,000 years ago, and it probably happened in a fertile river valley.

Before people became farmers, they had to gather fruit and berries or hunt animals for food. Farming began when people started to harvest wild wheat and oats. But it was a much bigger step to gather seeds, clear the ground and plant fields.

Instead of wandering, the first farmers had to stay in one place to tend their crops. They gave up hunting and, instead, kept herds of animals such as sheep, goats, pigs and cattle.

Farming was the beginning of civilization. Trade grew as farmers sold food to their neighbors. And, by cutting down trees and clearing the land to make fields, human beings began to change the appearance of the earth.

▼ WHERE WERE WHEELED CARTS FIRST USED?

In history, a few inventions have altered the course of civilization. Perhaps the most important of all engineering inventions was the wheel.

The wheel appears to have been invented in several parts of the Near East and Asia at roughly the same time – around 3000 BC. Perhaps the potter's wheel existed before the cart wheel.

Primitive people used sleds to drag loads. Someone must have thought of putting wooden rollers (such as tree branches) underneath the sled. This made it easier to pull. Fitting an axle, with wheels at each end, was a much more difficult step.

The first wheels were probably cut from tree trunks. They were solid and clumsy. Wheels with spokes came later, about 2000 BC.

To make full use of the wheel, an animal is needed to pull a cart. The first carts were pulled by people, but in time animals were trained for this work.

▼ WHERE DID PEOPLE FIRST USE WRITING?

Stone Age people "wrote" in pictures. In time, pictures were turned into "picture-signs." This was the beginning of writing.

About 6,000 years ago, people in Babylon, China and Egypt had learned to use picture-signs. They made marks in wet clay with their fingers or with sticks. A picture of the sun, for example, might mean "heat."

Later, people invented signs that stood for sounds or ideas, rather than pictures. The Sumerians, for example, used a cuneiform, or wedge-shaped, script. A stick was used for writing the marks on clay tablets. Some of the earliest written records are sums or tally marks made by clerks to keep count of goods or animals.

Around 1500 BC, the Phoenicians invented an alphabet based on sounds. From this come the alphabets we use today.

▼ WHERE WAS PAPER FIRST MADE?

Paper is the most common material used today for writing and printing on. It was unknown in ancient times until the Chinese invented a method of paper-making.

In ancient Egypt, people wrote on papyrus-reed scrolls. In Babylonia, they made marks on tablets of wet clay. The Romans wrote on sheets of parchment (very thin leather).

In about AD 100, the Chinese found out how to make thin sheets of paper from pulped fibers and rags. They kept the secret to themselves for hundreds of years.

Later, the Arabs discovered the secret and, much later, the art of paper-making spread to Europe. By the 1300s there were paper mills in France, Spain, Italy and Germany.

The invention of printing machines in the 1450s led to a great increase in the use of paper. Without paper, the rapid increase in book production, and the spread of knowledge that went with it, could not have taken place.

◄ WHERE WAS SILK FIRST PRODUCED?

Silk was first made in China. Threads from silkworm cocoons were spun on spinning wheels, then woven into fine cloth.

The Chinese found out how to make silk over 5,000 years ago. They guarded the secret, for silk was a rare fabric and very costly. Traders made the long journey along the "Silk Road" to buy Chinese silk, traveling from as far as India and the Middle East.

In AD 552 two Persian monks smuggled the secret of silk-making out of China. They hid silkworm eggs inside hollow bamboo canes, and also took seeds of the mulberry tree, whose leaves silkworms eat.

In time, people in Europe learned how to rear silkworms (the larvae of the silk moth) and to make silk. Silk was used to make fine, soft robes for rulers and nobles. To make silk, the delicate thread used by the silkworm to spin its cocoon must be unwound. As much as 1,000 feet may be unwound from one cocoon.

► WHERE WAS THE POTTER'S WHEEL INVENTED?

Pottery was one of the earliest inventions. At first, pots were shaped by hand out of wet clay. Turning pots on a wheel came later.

The wheel was invented in Sumeria, Babylon and elsewhere in the Near East around 3000 BC. Clay pots had already been made for over 5,000 years, but they were crude and often broke.

Making pots is a skillful craft. The potter needs skill not only in spinning the wheel to shape the pot, but also in firing the pot in a kiln to harden it. The first potters learned also how to glaze (coat) pots with various substances to make the pots stronger and more decorative.

The invention of the potter's wheel led to one of the first industries – pottery. A skillful potter could make enough pots to exchange them for food and other goods, or sell them for money.

◄ WHERE WERE THE FIRST OLYMPIC GAMES HELD?

Every four years, from 776 BC, the Greeks held a great festival. Artists, writers and athletes gathered to honor the great god Zeus. The contests were held at Olympia, and became known as the Olympic Games.

The first Olympic Games were not just sporting contests. There were plays and recitals by poets, as well as races. To the Greeks, the Games expressed the union of mind and body, striving for victory to honor Zeus, the king of the gods.

The events lasted for three days. Athletes ran, wrestled, rode horses and drove chariots. The Games began with the Olympic oath and ended with prizes and feasting.

The Olympic Games continued until AD 393. They were then forgotten until 1896, when they were revived at Athens on the suggestion of a Frenchman, Baron Pierre de Coubertin. They continue to be held every four years.

▶ WHERE DID THE GREEKS FOUND COLONIES?

The rulers of ancient Greece encouraged people to set off and found new colonies overseas. So Greek civilization spread far beyond its birthplace.

By the 8th century BC, Greece could no longer feed its growing population. The rulers of the Greek city-states feared discontent. So they were happy to see some of their citizens leave home to found new Greek colonies, where there was land for all.

Some Greek colonists went east to the Black Sea. But most journeyed west to Italy, Sicily and southern France. A few went as far as Africa, including Egypt.

Each Greek colony became a "little Greece" in a strange land. The Greek settlers traded for goods with the cities where they had once lived. In this way Greek skills and Greek ideas were carried to new cities all around the Mediterranean coast.

France
Spain
Italy
Greece
Black Sea
Sicily
Asia Minor
Mediterranean Sea
North Africa

◀ WHEN DID PEOPLE FIRST USE MONEY?

Today we use money to buy things. But when trade began thousands of years ago, there was no money. So people exchanged goods. The invention of money made trade much simpler.

The first metal coins were minted (made) in about 800 BC. Before then, all trade had been done by barter – that is, by exchanging goods. For example, a tool-maker might barter tools in exchange for meat or clothing.

As civilization developed, trade became more complex. Barter was a clumsy method. A trader needed small, easily carried tokens to exchange, but the tokens had to be valuable. So the first coins were made of metal, in particular gold and silver.

Gold coins have real value. Paper money, on the other hand, is merely a token. The paper itself is worthless. Paper money was invented in China, and was in use there by AD 800.

▶ WHERE WERE ROADS FIRST PAVED?

When people first began to travel, they followed rough tracks and trails. In bad weather, it was safer to stay at home. Paved roads were not thought of until wheeled carts came into use.

The earliest paved roads were made in Babylon some 4,000 years ago. As people began living in towns and trading with their neighbors, they needed better transport. A cart could not cross wild country, for fear of breaking an axle or sinking into mud or sand.

Many ancient cities had paved roads, and we can still see their remains today. But undoubtedly the greatest road-builders of the past were the Romans. Their roads ran straight from town to town.

Roman roads were built by army engineers. They were made of stones and gravel, and cambered (sloped) so that rain would drain away to the sides. Roman armies marched swiftly along these fine roads to keep the peace within the Roman Empire.

Drainage ditch
Stone slabs
Stone filling
Earth base
Stones and cement

▼ WHERE WAS THE PLOW INVENTED?

The first farmers tilled the soil with hand plows similar to garden hoes. It was in Mesopotamia, around 4000 BC, that farmers began using oxen to pull plows.

The plow was probably invented before the wheel. It began as a rough wooden tool, dragged up and down a field to scratch the surface of the soil. The farmer sowed seeds in the channel made by the plow.

Around 500 BC, a much improved plow appeared. It had a blade, or share, tipped with iron. And it was made in such a way that the blade turned the soil completely over, making a furrow.

In the Middle East, a small plow worked perfectly well. But larger plows were needed to tackle the heavy, hilly soils of northern Europe. Some plows were so heavy that they needed a team of up to eight oxen to pull them. Because the oxen could not turn sharply, fields became very large. Each field was divided into long strips, with drainage ditches in between.

▼ WHERE WERE ANIMALS FIRST USED FOR FARM WORK?

The first farmers worked with their hands, using simple tools. Training animals to pull plows and carts, as well as work machines, made the farmer's life much easier.

An ox is much stronger than a human. It can pull a heavier plow, and do more work in a day. The use of oxen to help with farm work dates from about 4000 BC in Mesopotamia, in the "fertile crescent" where farming began.

The animals that could be tamed in this way were herd animals such as cattle, asses, horses and camels. Oxen were harnessed with a wooden yoke across their necks. The yoke was not suitable for horses, however, and so horses were kept only for riding until much later, when the horse-collar harness was invented.

In the Middle East, animals were used to provide the power for simple machines, such as water pumps for irrigating fields. Animals were used everywhere to carry loads.

▼ WHERE DID THE FIRST KEY TURN IN A LOCK?

Once people had more than just one or two possessions, they needed a way of keeping property safe. The earliest locks were made in Egypt in about 2000 BC. They were clumsy, but they worked.

The locks invented by the ancient Egyptians were made of wood. The idea was simple. A door was kept shut by a bolt slid across the door and into a slot in the door frame. The bolt had several holes drilled in

it. When it was slid shut, pins in the lock dropped down into the holes. The bolt was then held fast.

To open the lock, the pins had to be lifted free. This was done with a key which was pushed into a hole in the bolt. Only the right key, with the right number of pegs cut into it, would fit.

The Egyptians took great trouble to secure the rich tombs of the pharaohs against thieves. Even so, many tombs were plundered and stripped of their treasures.

▼ WHERE WAS IRON FIRST SMELTED?

Iron must be heated in a furnace before it can be shaped to make tools. The secret of "smelting" iron was discovered in the Near East around 1500 BC.

As early as 4000 BC, people had learned to make tools and weapons from copper, which is a fairly soft metal. Copper can be hammered into shape when cold. In Sumeria, smiths found that copper and tin could be mixed to make bronze.

Iron is much stronger than copper or bronze. To smelt it, a very hot furnace is required. Ancient iron tools have been found at Ur of the Chaldees and inside Egyptian tombs. By 1200 BC iron had replaced copper and bronze.

Iron was thought to be magical, and the smiths who forged iron swords and spears were believed to have supernatural power. The Greeks valued iron as highly as gold. The Chinese, who invented efficient bellows to make furnaces very hot, made fine iron.

▼ WHERE WERE IRON WEAPONS FIRST USED IN WAR?

War in ancient times was fought at close range. But then, as now, the "arms race" was on. The first to use iron weapons were the Assyrians. They became the most feared of all.

The first real armies were those of Assyria and Egypt, some 3,000 years ago. Before then, wars were fought mainly by small groups of warriors. Egypt had many soldiers, but few wore any kind of protective clothing. Egyptian archers used reed arrows tipped with stone or copper.

Iron, the new metal, was harder and sharper. The Assyrians discovered how to use it in warfare. They made iron heads for their spears and arrows. For defense, the Assyrian soldiers wore long coats of iron chain mail.

Iron weapons were much stronger than weapons made of copper or bronze. Sword, spear, shield and armor could be made of iron, making the "iron warrior" much more formidable than his foes.

▼ WHERE WERE THE FIRST ROCKETS FIRED?

The Chinese invented the rocket. From this simple firework have come today's space rockets and missiles.

The first rockets were tubes filled with gunpowder (a mixture of potassium nitrate, charcoal and sulfur). The Chinese discovered thousands of years ago that gunpowder explodes when burned. Packed into a tube, the exploding gunpowder pushed out a stream of hot gas, sending the tube flying off in the opposite direction.

The Chinese let off fireworks for fun, but also fired rockets as weapons of war. In the Middle Ages, the invention spread to Europe. During the wars of the early 1800s the British army used rocket batteries to bombard Copenhagen in 1807 and during the battle of Leipzig in 1813.

The forerunner of the modern long-range rocket was the German V2. This was used during World War II.

▼ WHERE DID HOUSES FIRST HAVE CENTRAL HEATING?

Until the 20th century, most people in cold countries kept warm beside open fires. We think of central heating as a modern invention. In fact, the Romans had central heating 2,000 years ago.

The Romans were excellent builders. Their houses had proper drains and their towns had good water supplies. A wealthy Roman's house usually had underfloor heating too.

The heat came from a furnace. The floor was built on brick pillars so that hot air from the furnace could flow freely beneath it and up through pipes to rooms above. This system was known as a hypocaust. At the public baths, the hypocaust heated water for the hot pools and steam rooms. There Romans would meet to relax and enjoy a bath, and maybe a massage.

The Romans built central-heating systems throughout their empire. But after the Romans, the secret of the hypocaust was forgotten.

▼ WHERE DID ALEXANDER LEAD HIS ARMY?

Alexander, King of Macedonia, was a famous warrior. He was called "the Great" because he led his army to victory after victory.

Alexander was born in 356 BC. Macedonia was then a small kingdom in Greece. Becoming king at the age of 20, Alexander set out on an astonishing quest for power.

First, he conquered the other city-states of Greece. Then he took on the mighty

▲ WHERE DID THE ROMANS BUILD HUGE AQUEDUCTS?

An aqueduct is a bridge or channel built to carry drinking water into a city. The Romans built aqueducts so well that some still exist today.

Every Roman town needed a reliable water supply. Sometimes it was necessary to build an aqueduct to bring water from a nearby lake or river. The aqueduct was either a conduit (channel) or a huge bridge carrying a canal on top.

Persian Empire and defeated it. He invaded Egypt and founded the city of Alexandria.

Even then, his ambition was not satisfied. He led his army into India, but his troops were weary of conquest. They refused to march farther, and Alexander had to turn back.

In 12 years, Alexander was never defeated. He was only 33 when he died. After his death, his vast empire broke up. After Alexander, no other general could rule such a conquest.

Near Nîmes in France is an aqueduct built by the Roman general Agrippa. It has three stories, or tiers, raised on arches. The longest aqueduct was over 53 miles long. One of the most famous was called the Aqua Appia. It was built in 312 BC to carry water into Rome, and was about 10 miles long. Nearby ran the road called the Via Appia, or Appian Way. Both were built by the Roman military engineer Appius Claudius Caecus.

▼ WHERE DID THE ROMAN EMPIRE END?

The Roman Empire was the greatest of ancient times. Rome's rule stretched from Britain in the west to the Black Sea in the east. Its empire lasted for 500 years.

Rome began as a small kingdom in what is now Italy. The Romans first conquered Italy (by 200 BC), then the other Mediterranean lands and North Africa. They eventually ruled most of western and central Europe.

Augustus became the first Roman emperor in 27 BC. Roman rule brought peace to the conquered lands. But the Roman armies were faced with attacks from barbarians living beyond the Empire.

In AD 476 the barbarians captured Rome. By then the Empire was weak and divided. Only in the East, with its capital at Constantinople, did the Roman Empire survive. The Eastern Empire lasted until Constantinople fell to the Turks in 1453.

▼ WHERE WERE THE FIRST UNIVERSITIES FOUNDED?

A university is a place of "all learning." New knowledge in the Middle Ages led to the setting up of great centers of learning throughout Europe. Many of these universities are still in existence today.

By the 1300s, knowledge was growing rapidly. For centuries education had been left to the Church. Now, all over Europe, universities came into being.

Great universities were founded in cities such as Paris, Bologna, Oxford, Cambridge and Prague. The only subjects taught at first were law, theology (religion) and medicine. One of the first medical schools was founded in the 9th century at the university of Salerno in Italy.

Each university was granted a royal charter. This gave it privileges and the right to award degrees to its students. Scholars from all over Europe taught at the universities. They taught in Latin, the "universal language." Today there are universities in many countries, teaching a variety of subjects.

▼ WHERE HAS THE MOST ANCIENT BIBLE BEEN FOUND?

In 1947 a goatherd came across some ancient scrolls in a cave close to the Dead Sea. These scrolls contain parts of the Bible written perhaps 200 years before the birth of Christ.

The Dead Sea Scrolls caused great interest among scholars. Reading and preserving the scrolls required much patience and careful work. The scrolls had been rolled inside jars for

safekeeping, and they had to be unrolled with great care.

Almost every book of the Old Testament appears, at least in fragments, in the scrolls. The oldest passages from the Book of Leviticus, were written in an early Canaanite form of Hebrew.

The scrolls were probably stored in the caves by Jews at the time when Palestine was ruled by Rome. The hot, dry desert air helped to preserve the fragile scrolls. From them we have learned much about how the Bible came to be written.

▶ WHERE DID MUHAMMAD FLEE?

The religion of Islam was founded by the Prophet Muhammad. In AD 622 he had to flee from his home in Mecca to Medina.

Muhammad was born in about AD 570 in Mecca, in present-day Saudi Arabia. At the age of 40 he set out to call people to a belief in one God.

Muhammad was persecuted when he began preaching. With a few followers, he was forced to flee from Mecca to Medina. His flight is known as the Hegira, and the Islamic calendar is dated from it. For some years there was war between the Meccans and the followers of Muhammad. In 630, Muhammad captured Mecca.

The words of God, as revealed to Muhammad, were written down in the Koran, and the religion he founded grew to be one of the great faiths. To Muslims (followers of Islam), Mecca and Medina are holy places.

▶ WHICH EUROPEAN CITY WAS THE CAPITAL OF AN ISLAMIC EMPIRE?

The Moors were a Muslim people of North Africa. They created a large empire, which included part of Spain, and made Seville their capital. The Moors took Islamic art, science and learning to Europe.

The Moors originally lived on the Barbary Coast of North Africa. They were converted to Islam in AD 707. At this time Islam was growing fast, and the Moors took part in this expansion.

They invaded Spain, and remained powerful there for hundreds of years. They made Seville, their capital city, a centre of Islamic culture. Islamic civilization was more advanced than that of medieval Europe, especially in the fields of science and medicine.

Christian leaders fought against the Moors. Gradually, the power of the Moors weakened. In 1238 they retired to Granada, the last Moorish kingdom in Europe, and were eventually driven out in 1492.

◀ WHERE WAS CATHAY?

Before the 13th century, Europeans knew little of Asia. To them, Cathay (China) was an unknown land. No Europeans had been there until the Polo family made their journeys.

Chinese civilization was the oldest on earth, but the Chinese cared little about the world outside. In Europe, only a few fantastic stories of "Cathay" were known.

In 1260, the brothers Niccolo and Maffeo Polo set out from Venice to trade in the East. They returned in 1269 with tales of their visit to Cathay, where they had met its Mongol ruler, Kublai Khan.

In 1271 they left Venice once more. With them went Niccolo's son, Marco. The overland journey to China took four years. The Polos did not return to Venice until 1295. Marco traveled throughout China in the service of Kublai Khan. When he returned, Marco wrote a book about his travels. From it, Europeans discovered that they had much to learn from the Chinese.

▲ WHERE DID EUROPE GET SPICES FROM IN THE MIDDLE AGES?

For people in medieval Europe, winter was a hard time. There was little food for farm animals, so most were killed in autumn. **Spices were used to preserve and flavor meat during the winter. These spices came from Asia.**

The need to disguise the bad taste of rotten meat led Europeans to explore the oceans. This is strange, but true, for the spices the Europeans needed came from the Spice Islands, in what are now the East Indies.

The journey overland was long, with the result that spices were very costly. In the 1400s, Europeans searched for new sea routes to the Indies.

When Columbus landed in the New World in 1492, he hoped he had reached the Spice Islands. He was wrong. But the quest for spices had led to the discovery of a vast new continent.

◄ WHERE WAS THE FIRST BOOK PRINTED?

The Chinese were the first people to print books on paper. They used wood blocks for this. Much later, the mechanical printing press was invented.

The earliest known printed book was made around AD 868. It is called the *Diamond Sutra* and was hand-printed, using wooden blocks. This printing method is slow. Even so, it is faster than copying books by hand. In Europe, at that time, all books were copied by hand – usually by monks. Books were so precious that they were often chained to reading stands.

In the 1400s, a German known as Johannes Gutenberg invented a printing machine. This used separate pieces of metal type for each letter. The letters were arranged in order to make up a whole page of words. This was then printed by a screw-type press. The printing press made it possible to print books in much larger numbers.

► WHERE DID THE LONGBOW PROVE TO BE DECISIVE IN WARFARE?

In the Middle Ages, the longbow was the main "long-range" weapon. Often it was the archers who decided the outcome of a battle.

In 1337, England and France went to war. The war lasted more than a hundred years. In 1346, the English army won the battle of Crécy. The English success owed much to their skill with the longbow. In 1415, English and Welsh archers won another battle, at Agincourt.

The longbow was powerful and accurate. With it, an archer could bring down a knight on horseback. The longbow could be shot more rapidly than its rival, the crossbow. Medieval kings encouraged archery as a sport, to ensure that there would be a ready supply of trained bowmen for use in war.

Archers were also carried on warships. Many longbows have been found in the wreck of the English ship *Mary Rose*, which sank in 1545.

Bering Strait

Asia

North America

Route from Asia to North America

◄ WHERE DID THE AMERICAN INDIANS COME FROM?

When Columbus discovered America he thought he had reached the Indies, in Asia. So he called the people "Indians." Columbus was wrong. But the American Indians had in fact come from Asia thousands of years earlier.

The American Indians look a bit like the Mongols who still live in eastern Asia. The Indians crossed a "land bridge" to reach North America. Today, the two continents are separated by a channel of sea called the Bering Strait.

The Indians began settling in America about 25,000 years ago. They lived by hunting and farming. There were many groups, or tribes, and each had its own customs and beliefs.

The Indians had to travel on foot, since the horses which had once lived in America had died out before the Indians arrived. It was the Spanish who re-introduced horses to America in the 1500s.

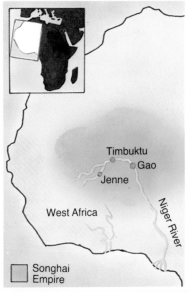

Timbuktu
Gao
Jenne

West Africa

Niger River

Songhai Empire

◄ WHERE WAS THE SONGHAI EMPIRE?

In the 1500s there was a rich and powerful empire in West Africa. This was the empire of the Songhai, who were soldiers, farmers and traders.

The Songhai Empire included lands in the countries we now call Mali, Niger and Nigeria. The Songhai people controlled the trade and fishing along the great Niger River. From around AD 800, they played an important part in West African events. The Songhai kings challenged the Islamic rulers of the Mali Empire farther north. For many years there was war.

The Songhai grew rich on the salt and gold trades. They controlled the caravan routes to the north. Their downfall came in the late 1500s. Already weakened by squabbles between its princes, Songhai was attacked by Moroccan armies. The Moroccans had firearms and, with the help of these new weapons, captured the important Songhai towns of Gao and Timbuktu.

◄ WHERE WAS EL DORADO SUPPOSED TO BE?

El Dorado **is Spanish for "the golden one." Early explorers in South America heard strange tales of a land so rich that its ruler bathed in gold dust.**

We now use the expression "El Dorado" to mean an imaginary country full of riches. But the tales the early Spanish adventurers heard, as they explored South America in the 1500s, told of a man, not just a country.

El Dorado was said to be the chief of a tribe living in a marvelous city called Omoa. Each year, as part of a great sacred festival, the chief bathed in gold dust, for the land was so rich that gold was as plentiful as water.

El Dorado was supposed to live somewhere in what is now Colombia. None of the Spanish explorers who went in search of his fabulous land ever discovered it. But they did find plenty of gold elsewhere in South America.

▶ WHERE DID THE PILGRIM FATHERS LAND?

In November, 1620, a small ship landed in North America. It was called the *Mayflower*. On board were some 35 settlers from England, remembered today as the Pilgrim Fathers.

The Europe from which the Pilgrim Fathers came was torn by religious quarrels. The Pilgrim Fathers wanted peace to set up a church of their own, so they decided to risk the perilous two-month voyage across the ocean to America.

The Pilgrim Fathers planned to sail in two ships. But when one proved unsafe, all the passengers crowded aboard the *Mayflower*. The sea voyage was stormy but they reached America and settled where Plymouth, Massachusetts, now stands.

Half of the settlers died during the first winter. But the colony survived to harvest its first crops in November 1621. This is remembered in the United States today as Thanksgiving Day.

▶ WHERE DID A TEA PARTY START A REVOLUTION?

The colonists of America were tired of old ways. They wanted to govern themselves. When Britain tried to tax its colonies in America, the colonists protested. The American Revolution followed.

By the mid-1700s there were 13 British colonies in America. The colonies made their own local laws but the British government kept control of money and trade.

In 1763, the British also gained control of French territory in North America. To raise money for stationing troops there, the British government tried to tax the colonists. One of the taxes was on tea.

The Americans protested. In 1773 a group of colonists crept on to a ship in Boston harbor. Disguised as Indians, they threw its cargo of tea into the water. The "Boston Tea Party" began a revolution, leading to American independence in 1783.

▶ WHERE DID THE OPIUM WAR BREAK OUT?

The war of 1840-42 between Great Britain and China is called the Opium War. It started when the Chinese government tried to stop Europeans from importing the illegal drug opium into China.

For hundreds of years China had tried to keep out foreign traders, but Europeans were eager to profit from the trade in opium, a drug which was smoked in pipes.

The Chinese government tried to end this trade, and destroyed the British merchants' stocks of opium. The British declared war and attacked China.

The Opium War ended in 1842 with the Treaty of Nanking. This opened five ports in China to British trade, and handed over Hong Kong to Britain. China was also forced to pay damages to the British merchants.

This began a period of foreign domination of China, which was to be the cause of the later Boxer Rebellion.

▶ WHERE DID AMERICAN SLAVES FOUND A FREE COUNTRY?

During the 1700s many Africans were taken to work as slaves in America. In 1822 a homeland for freed slaves was set up in Africa. Its name was Liberia.

In America, rich white people owned many black slaves. But others fought to end the evil of slavery. This struggle eventually led to the US Civil War (1861-65).

A few black slaves won their freedom before the Civil War, but they were homeless. They decided to return to Africa, the land from which their ancestors had been taken in the slave ships.

Liberia, the land of freedom, was founded in 1822. Its capital, Monrovia, was named after President James Monroe.

Today, Liberia is an independent republic. Many of its citizens can trace their ancestry back to those first settlers who made the return journey from America to Africa.

◀ WHERE DID THE BOXER REBELLION TAKE PLACE?

In the 1890s powerful European countries controlled much of China's trade. The Chinese uprising against this unfair control is known as the Boxer Rebellion.

The "Boxers" were members of a patriotic secret society called the "Society of the Righteous and Harmonious Fists." They were angered to see China falling more and more under foreign influence.

In 1900 the Boxers rose in rebellion to drive out the foreigners. The Empress Dowager, Tzu-hsi, encouraged the rebels.

In the capital, Peking, the Europeans took refuge inside their embassies. The siege of Peking lasted 55 days before an international army entered the city to rescue the Europeans.

After the Boxer Rebellion, the Europeans demanded that China pay compensation. The Boxers had failed; but they had shown how weak the Chinese emperors had become. In 1911 China became a republic.

▶ WHERE DID TANKS FIRST PLAY A PART IN WARFARE?

World War I was a war of terrible machines. Trench warfare killed thousands of soldiers. In 1916 a strange new weapon crawled into battle – the tank.

The generals could not understand the new warfare. As whole armies became bogged down in the muddy trenches of Europe's battlefields, they looked for a breakthrough. Cavalry had been made out of date by barbed wire and machine guns. A new weapon was needed.

In the summer of 1916, during the battle of the Somme, the British introduced the first tanks. They were armored tractors, crawling on caterpillar tracks, firing cannon and machine guns. Not even a trench could halt them.

They were sent into battle singly, to help soldiers on foot. Only a few people saw that the tank's future lay in mass onslaughts. This was proved in World War II when German tank armies swept across much of Europe in a few weeks.

◄ WHERE DID THE LEAGUE OF NATIONS MEET?

After the slaughter of World War I, many nations sought a lasting peace. The League of Nations was set up in 1920 with the aim of settling quarrels peacefully. The League met at Geneva, in Switzerland, but it was doomed to fail.

The League of Nations was meant to act as a world council, but it had no real powers. The leader who did the most to bring the League into existence was Woodrow Wilson, the U.S. President. Wilson, however, could not persuade officials to join the League. Other states, such as Germany, left the League as soon as their own behavior was criticized.

The League could not prevent the world slipping into another war in 1939. It had failed. In 1945, the United Nations Organization was set up, with similar aims. The UN has been more successful, but still lacks the power to be a true "world government."

► WHERE WERE THE FIRST ATOMIC BOMBS DROPPED?

World War II was nearly over by 1945, but Japan fought on. To end the war, a terrible new weapon was used: the atomic bomb.

During World War II, both sides worked to make an atomic bomb. Scientists from many countries gathered in the United States. There the first atom bomb was tested on 16 July, 1945.

By 1945, Germany was defeated but Japan was still fighting. To land armies in Japan would have been slow and costly. So the Allies decided to use their new weapon. On 6 August, 1945, an atomic bomb was dropped on the Japanese city of Hiroshima. On 9 August, a second bomb was dropped on Nagasaki.

Both cities were destroyed. Over 100,000 people were killed and an equal number were injured. The war was over, but the world now feared the terrible destructive power of the atomic bomb.

◄ WHERE WAS THE SIX-DAY WAR FOUGHT?

The state of Israel came into being in 1948. Since then, Israel has fought several wars with neighboring Arab countries. In 1967, the Israelis won a war in just six days.

Israel was founded in what had been Palestine. The Jews had long dreamed of a homeland, a reborn Israel. But the Arabs living in Palestine and neighboring states opposed this idea.

After World War II, many Jewish people went to live in Palestine. The homeland was declared and in 1948 the state of Israel came into existence. At once there was war between Israel and its neighbors.

Israel has fought many wars since 1948. In 1967, Israel fought both Egypt and Jordan. The Israeli armies, helped by air attacks, won a rapid victory in six days. Israel captured the west bank of the River Jordan and seized much Egyptian territory in Gaza and Sinai.

PEOPLE AND PLACES

▼ WHERE DO PEOPLE LIVE IN TENTS?

Most tent-dwellers are nomads of West and Central Asia. Nomads need homes that they can move from place to place because they have to wander with their flocks and herds to find fresh pastures.

Famous tent-dwelling nomads include the Bedouin of Arabia. These desert-dwellers live in long, low tents that are made of black goats'-hair cloth held up by poles and ropes pegged in the sand. One strip of cloth serves as the roof. Another strip protects one side from the wind. Bedouin tents are light to carry and easy to erect.

The Kazaks and Mongolians of Central Asia use another kind of tent – the *ger* or *yurt*. Yurts look more like portable huts than tents. They consist of thick layers of felt laid over a wooden frame, with an outer covering of hide or canvas. Strong and gale-proof, yurts keep out the bitterly cold winds that sweep across Central Asia in winter.

▼ WHERE DO PEOPLE LIVE IN WOODEN HOUSES?

Wooden houses are found mostly in areas where there is plenty of timber, for example, North America, northern Europe and the Far East.

In Europe people build wooden houses among the mountains of lands such as Austria, Germany, Switzerland, Norway and Sweden. Mountain chalets are made of pine or fir logs. These have heavy timbers and broad overhanging roofs.

European settlers took their building skills to North America. They made log cabins roofed with bark, thatch or wooden tiles called shingles. Today many American and Canadian homes have a timber frame and outer walls made of overlapping wooden planks.

Bedouin tent

Mongolian yurts

▼ WHERE DO PEOPLE LIVE IN HOUSES ON STILTS?

There are several parts of the world where you might see houses built on stilts. These are where people have raised homes over shallow water, or on land likely to be flooded.

Many stilt houses stand in shallow, sheltered coastal waters in Southeast Asia or on Pacific Ocean islands. Strong, long wooden posts (piles), driven deep down into mud, form a firm foundation for these buildings.

Fishing villages of pile dwellings rise from lagoons in the Philippine Islands. These homes have wooden floors and walls, and steep, thatched roofs. People build other kinds of wooden-framed pile dwellings on Polynesian islands, in New Guinea, along the Amazon River, and on lagoons in West African countries such as Benin.

Stilt houses have been built for thousands of years. In Italy and Switzerland there are remains of pile dwellings which stood on the shores of lakes in Bronze-Age times.

▼ WHERE DO PEOPLE LIVE IN MUD HOUSES?

People build mud houses mostly in lands where mud is a more plentiful material than wood or stone, and where there is hot sunshine to bake the soft mud hard.

Many African peoples build huts with walls made of mud. In the Sudan, some Nuba families each have a cluster of five round mud huts with thatched roofs. One hut serves as a bedroom, another is a barn, and so on. In northern Nigeria people build mud houses that have straight walls and a flat roof.

Unusual mud homes outside Africa include the beehive-shaped mud houses built by Arabs in the Syrian Desert. In Mexico and the southwestern United States there are so-called adobe houses. These are made from mud that has been mixed with straw, and then shaped into bricks and left in the sun to dry.

Few houses are built of mud in climates that are wet or cold. Rain and frost would soon wash away the mud or make it crumble into dust.

▼ WHERE DO PEOPLE LIVE ON BOATS?

In the Western world some people live on barges and flat-bottomed boats called houseboats. But most of the world's boat-dwellers live in East Asia on craft that are much smaller.

Most boat-dwellers live in China, Japan and nearby islands. Many Chinese people spend their lives on boats moored just off the overcrowded island of Hong Kong. Where there is no space to build a home on land, or the land is too expensive, thousands of families have no choice but to live on water.

In Hong Kong harbor and the big Chinese rivers, most boat-dwellers live on light craft called sampans. A sampan usually has a small cabin with a roof made of mats. Inside, a whole family will cook, eat, work and sleep.

Life is cramped. Sometimes it is dangerous as well. Tropical storms and huge waves set off by earthquakes can sink sampans moored in shallow seas, or drive boats ashore.

79

◀ WHERE CAN STONE-AGE PEOPLE STILL BE FOUND?

Some peoples still live an almost Stone-Age way of life in several of the world's wild places. These include Africa's Kalahari Desert, the Amazon Forest of Brazil and the island of New Guinea. But the most primitive people of all are the Tasaday of Mindanao, an island in the Philippines.

Scientists first visited the Tasaday in 1971. They found 25 Tasaday people living in a cave halfway up a wooded hill. The Tasaday make and use stone tools and fire, but their only clothes are leaves. They eat crabs, fish and tadpoles. The Tasaday catch these by feeling for them under rocks in mountain streams. They also collect and cook wild plants.

The Tasaday are peaceful people and get on well together. There is no single leader of the group. One scientist thought they were the gentlest people on earth. Perhaps our early Stone-Age ancestors led lives much like those of the Tasaday.

▶ WHERE DO THE MASAI LIVE?

The Masai are a group of African cattle-keeping people. They live east of Lake Victoria in the highlands of Kenya and Tanzania.

The equator crosses Masai territory from east to west, and the Great Rift Valley runs from north to south.

Masai are tall and slim with a high, narrow head and slender hands and feet. Most live in villages of mud-and-brushwood huts set in a circle. Family groups consist of a man, his wives and their children. Young men become warriors and live in separate villages.

Most Masai eat mainly maize and millet, but warriors feed on milk and blood. They obtain blood by cutting a vein in the neck of a cow or bullock. The cut later heals. Masai also kill sheep for food, but eat cattle only if these die of injury or illness. Warriors with spears and shields guard the herds. They may also raid the cattle of their neighbors.

◀ WHERE DO BUSHMEN LIVE?

Bushmen live in the Kalahari Desert, a barren part of southwest Africa. Some still hunt and gather food, as all people used to in the Old Stone Age.

The ancestors of Bushmen lived in much of southern Africa until they were driven out by other Africans. Today the Bushmen live in the Kalahari Desert, an open waste with little water and few trees.

Bushmen are small, slight people with yellow-brown skin and tightly curled hair. They keep no animals and grow no crops, but they are skillful hunters. Bushmen imitate the cries of wild beasts to lure their prey nearer. They kill antelope with bows and arrows, and set snares for smaller beasts.

Women gather edible insects, roots and berries. Bushmen know how to find juicy bulbs and how to use a reed to suck up moisture from wet sand. They can survive where most people would quickly die of thirst or hunger.

► WHERE DO SHERPAS LIVE?

Sherpas are a group of hardy people who live in Nepal, a kingdom north of India among the towering Himalaya Mountains.

Sherpas live in the Khumba Valley of northeast Nepal, close to the world's highest peak, Mount Everest. They grow grain and potatoes and keep sheep and cattle.

Sherpas are a sturdy people related to the Tibetans farther north. Many belong to the Buddhist faith. They are well known as the hard-working porters who carry loads for mountain climbers in the Himalayas. Sherpas can carry immensely heavy loads on their backs all day. What is more, they can work at heights where most people would feel dizzy and faint.

The most famous of all the Sherpas is Tenzing Norgay. With the New Zealand climber, Edmund Hillary, Tenzing Norgay became one of the first two people to reach the top of Mount Everest, in June 1953.

◄ WHERE DO THE AINU LIVE?

The Ainu are a people who live on certain islands in the northwest Pacific Ocean. Most live in Japan, but they do not closely resemble other Japanese people.

Some Ainu inhabit remote parts of Japan's large northern island, Hokkaido. Others live nearby on the Kurile Islands and Sakhalin Island in the Soviet Union. Many live in fishing villages.

In certain ways, the Ainu seem to resemble people of European rather than Japanese ancestry. Their bodies are heavily built and covered with much hair. Also, their hair is brown, not black like the hair of most of the peoples of East Asia. Some experts think that the Ainu are descended from an ancient group that once lived in much of Asia.

The Ainu had their own language, lived by fishing and hunting, and worshiped spirits. They wore clothes of skin or bark-cloth. But their old customs are now disappearing.

► WHERE DO GYPSIES COME FROM?

Gypsies are a wandering people found in many parts of the world. Their English name is short for "Egyptian," but their true home was probably India.

Many experts believe that gypsy travelers wandered west from India about six hundred years ago. They went through Iran and reached Syria and Egypt. By the 1500s some had reached Europe. Many entered Romania, Hungary, Russia, France, Spain and England. A few even crossed the sea to North America.

Thousands of gypsies still spend their lives wandering. They live in caravans and find work as traders, metalworkers or musicians. Some work in fairs; others deal in horses or used cars.

Gypsies tend to have dark skin, dark wavy hair, and big black or brown eyes. Many speak Romany, a language that comes from an ancient Indian tongue. Gypsies enjoy dancing and singing. They keep to their old traditions.

▶ WHERE DO ABORIGINES LIVE?

Aborigines are a country's earliest inhabitants. The best-known aborigines are those of Australia.

Australian Aborigines have dark-brown skin and wavy hair. Their ancestors may have migrated from Southeast Asia about 40,000 years ago.

Aborigines lived in small wandering bands and made simple shelters at resting places. They used weapons and tools made from wood and stone to hunt and gather food. One of their weapons was the boomerang. This is a throwing weapon made from wood. One type is cleverly designed to return to the thrower.

Australian Aborigines had their own music, art and religion. At times they would gather for a corroboree, a festival of music and dancing.

There were about 300,000 Aborigines in Australia when Europeans first arrived there two hundred years ago. Many Aborigines were persecuted by European settlers, and now only about 110,000 remain.

◀ WHERE DO MAORIS LIVE?

The Maoris are the native people of New Zealand. Indeed the word *Maori* means "native."

Maoris mostly have light-brown skin, brown or black hair and eyes, a broad face with high cheekbones, and a straight nose. They tend to be tall and strongly built.

Maoris speak a Polynesian language. Hundreds of years ago their ancestors sailed from far-off Pacific islands in huge canoes. They were the first people to discover and settle in New Zealand.

When British settlers arrived in the early 1800s, Maoris were Stone Age farmers, hunters and fishermen. They were skilled carvers, tattooists and weavers, and sang songs and war chants.

Maoris could be fierce warriors. At times their tribes fought British settlers. But later both groups made peace and intermarried. Maoris now lead a modern way of life but they keep up their customs. The Maoris shown here are wearing traditional dress.

▶ WHERE DO THE TUAREG LIVE?

The Tuareg are nomads of northern Africa. Some roam the Sahara Desert. Others live on its southern edge.

The Tuareg belong to the Berber peoples, who lived in North Africa long before the Arabs arrived. They speak the old Tuareg language and use an ancient kind of writing. The Tuareg are Muslims. In contrast to many Muslims, the Tuareg men, not the women, veil their faces.

There are two Tuareg classes: nobles and vassals. Nobles own camels, goats, sheep and farms set in oases. Vassals mind the nobles' livestock. Negro serfs grow crops on the nobles' farms.

Tuareg are independent and proud. They once raided and traded far across the Sahara. They also fought against the French Foreign Legion. But many Tuareg have now left the desert to find more fertile land to the south. Their old ways of life are vanishing fast.

◄ WHERE DO PYGMIES LIVE?

Pygmies are very small people, mostly living a primitive life. Groups live in remote parts of Africa, the Andaman Islands of the Indian Ocean, Malaysia and the Philippines. Their numbers are few and becoming fewer still.

The best-known pygmies are the African pygmies, known as Negrillos. These live in the hot, steamy forests of Central Africa. Negrillos look very like small Negroes. A full-grown Negrillo is no taller than a 10-year-old child of normal height.

African pygmies gather wild plants, catch fish, and use poisoned arrows to shoot animals such as monkeys and antelopes. They do not grow crops or keep farm animals.

Negrillos wear few clothes, but make bags and pottery and build simple huts. They are wanderers, but each small group has its own territory. Negrillos trade meat for iron tools and food grown by various tribes in the forest.

► WHERE DO ESKIMOS LIVE?

Eskimos live in the cold polar regions of North America and northeast Asia. They are related to the Chinese and Japanese. Their ancestors probably migrated across the Arctic thousands of years ago.

Eskimos are well built to survive long cold, Arctic winters. Their short, stocky bodies store heat better than those of tall, thin people.

Eskimos have learned how to cope with the cold. They make warm fur coats and build turf-roofed homes, half hidden underground. In winter, hunters far out on the ice build snow houses called igloos.

Eskimos are skilled at fishing and hunting seals and whales. Their hunting boats are slim, skin-covered canoes called *kayaks*. On land, teams of dogs haul sleds that carry equipment and dead game. But old ways of life are dying. Many Eskimos now live in wooden houses in towns.

◄ WHERE DO LAPPS LIVE?

Lapps live mostly in the region of northern Europe called Lapland. This covers parts of northern Sweden, Finland, and the USSR.

Lapps are short, strongly built people. They have straight black hair, low foreheads, and high cheekbones. Many have flat noses and thin lips. Lapps have their own language. They wear colorful clothes of wool and reindeer skins.

Different groups live in different places. Mountain Lapps lead a wandering life with their reindeer herds. Each family shares one tent.

River Lapps live a more settled life along river banks. Besides reindeer, they keep cattle and sheep. River Lapps hunt and fish, and some grow a few crops. Sea Lapps live in wood and turf huts built on the coast. Most work as fishermen.

The Lapps' ancestors lived in Central Asia. They reached Lapland thousands of years ago. Some Lapps now move out of Lapland and marry people to the south.

◄ WHERE HAVE ANCIENT TEMPLES BEEN DISMANTLED AND REBUILT?

When the High Dam was built at Aswan on the River Nile, a great lake formed behind it. To prevent the water engulfing them, two temples at Abu Simbel were dismantled and rebuilt on higher ground.

The Egyptian Pharaoh Ramses II had the temples built at Abu Simbel about 3,200 years ago. They were carved out of the face of a cliff beside the River Nile. The Great Temple had 14 rooms and stretched 197 feet into the cliff. Four huge stone seated figures of Ramses II flanked the entrance. Six huge figures guarded the other temple.

In the 1960s, the new Aswan High Dam blocked the Nile and its waters rose. To save the temples, workmen cut them into huge blocks weighing 20 to 30 tons each. They raised these to the nearby hilltop, then fitted them together again. About 50 nations gave money to pay for this colossal project.

◄ WHERE IS THE VALLEY OF THE KINGS?

This is a narrow rocky gorge in southern Egypt. Ancient Egyptians buried many of their kings in the valley.

The Valley of the Kings lies on the west bank of the Nile River, near the ancient Egyptian city of Thebes. Here, in the desert, people have discovered more than 60 tombs. They were made more than 3,200 years ago.

Each tomb consists of corridors and rooms cut deep into solid rock. Sculptors and artists carved and painted religious signs and writing on the walls. When a king died, people laid his body here inside a great stone coffin. They also left rich treasures for his use in an after-life.

Tombs had secret doors and deep pits to keep out robbers. In time, though, thieves plundered almost every tomb. Only one tomb remained intact. It belonged to Tutankhamun, a young, unimportant king, yet its splendor astonished the archaeologists who found it.

◄ WHERE IS THE BIGGEST ROMAN AMPHITHEATER?

The biggest ancient Roman amphitheater is the Colosseum in Rome, Italy. Amphitheaters were early sports stadiums. They had a central arena surrounded by seats. Indeed, their name means "theater on both sides."

The remains of the Colosseum still stand near the center of Rome. Its outer walls are 160 feet high, and it measures 614 feet in length and 515 feet in width.

More than 86,000 spectators could sit or stand on tiers raised on arches. They looked down on a big oval central arena. Engineers could flood this for sea battles. But the Romans used it mostly for fights to the death between trained fighters called gladiators, or between people and wild animals.

The Romans built the Colosseum by AD 80. Its name came later from a colossus (a huge statue) of the Emperor Nero. The Emperor Hadrian had this placed at the entrance.

▶ **WHERE WERE PYRAMIDS DISCOVERED IN THE JUNGLE?**

Since the late 1700s, explorers have found many ancient ruined pyramids in the forests of Central America. American Indians had built the pyramids centuries earlier.

Old stone pyramids stand in parts of Mexico, Belize, Guatemala, El Salvador and Honduras. They were used as temples. Most had flights of steps that led up to a small room on top. Here, priests used to sacrifice animals or people to their gods.

The first of these pyramids were built more than 3,000 years ago. Some are the largest (but not the tallest) pyramids on earth. Pyramid builders included peoples such as the Zapotecs, Mixtecs, Mayas, Toltecs and Aztecs.

In time, the pyramids and nearby towns were abandoned. This probably happened when the land around no longer produced enough crops or water to meet the needs of the people.

▶ **WHERE IS THE LOST CITY OF THE INCAS?**

The lost city of the Incas is Machu Picchu in the Andes Mountains of Peru. It is called "lost" because the Incas abandoned it, and the city remained unknown to explorers for several centuries.

Machu Picchu stands only 50 miles northwest of the city of Cuzco. But it is perched on a narrow mountain ridge about 6,760 feet above sea level. Forests hide it from below.

This is why it stayed forgotten until the American explorer Hiram Bingham rediscovered it in 1911. Bingham found houses, temples, and a hundred stairways. All were built of huge, well-fitting blocks of uncemented stone.

Bingham named the ruins Machu Picchu ("Old Peak") after a nearby mountain. But the Inca name seems to have been Vilcabamba. In 1580, the last Inca ruler of Peru may have fled to Machu Picchu to escape the Spanish who had seized the Inca Empire.

▶ **WHERE IS ANGKOR WAT?**

Angkor Wat is a great temple which was built by the Khmer people of Southeast Asia. It lies in Kampuchea, a country also known as Cambodia.

Angkor Wat means "city temple." This temple is the largest religious building in the world. Its outer wall encloses an area larger than a dozen football fields.

Inside stand several stone enclosures, each taller than the one outside it. In the middle rise five huge stone towers shaped like lotus flowers. Sheets of beaten gold once covered them. The middle tower is tallest, so the whole temple is shaped like a vast pyramid. Carvings on the walls of corridors show scenes from stories about Vishnu, a Hindu god.

A Khmer king, Suryavarman II, had Angkor Wat built in the early 1100s. Later, it was abandoned. A Frenchman, Henri Mouhot, discovered the overgrown ruins in the early 1860s.

▼ WHICH IS A HOLY CITY FOR THREE RELIGIONS?

Jerusalem is a holy city for people who belong to the religions of Judaism, Christianity and Islam. Jerusalem was once split between Jordan and Israel. In 1967 Israel seized all of it.

People of different faiths consider Jerusalem holy for different reasons. For the Jews, it was their ancient Hebrew capital, where King Solomon built the Temple. For Christians, the city is important because Jesus preached and died there.

Muslims believe that the Prophet Muhammad rose to heaven from a rock in Jerusalem. A beautiful shrine, known as the Dome of the Rock, now stands over the rock.

The Western (Wailing) Wall is especially holy to the Jews. Many Christians believe that the Church of the Holy Sepulchre marks the place where Jesus was buried. The picture shows the Dome of the Rock and the Wailing Wall in front of it. Jews gather at the Wall to pray.

▼ WHERE IS THE WAILING WALL?

The Wailing Wall, or Western Wall, is a high wall in eastern Jerusalem. It is one of the oldest, holiest places in Jewish history.

Today the wall forms part of the boundary of a Muslim sanctuary which includes the Dome of the Rock. The wall's proper name is the Western Wall. Some of it seems to be the remains of the western part of a far older wall. This surrounded the great Temple founded by King Solomon nearly 3,000 years ago. The Temple has been destroyed and rebuilt several times. The Romans destroyed the last Temple in AD 70.

The Wailing Wall is about 160 feet long and about 40 feet high. Its huge blocks of stone are built up in 28 layers. Only the lowest probably date back to the time of Solomon. Jews pray at the wall. They bewail the fall of the Temple and other disasters that befell their people long ago. They also pray to God for help in the future.

▲ WHERE IS THE CENTER OF THE ROMAN CATHOLIC CHURCH?

The Roman Catholic Church has its center at Vatican City, in Italy's capital, Rome. The Vatican Palace is the home of the Pope, the head of the Roman Catholic Church.

The Pope reigns from Rome because Roman Catholics believe that St. Peter made Rome the center of the early Christian Church. Catholics believe that Christ chose Peter to be the head of the Church on earth. They think of St. Peter as the first bishop of Rome, and the popes as St. Peter's successors.

St. Peter is thought to lie buried in the Vatican, under St. Peter's Basilica (shown here). This is the world's largest church. It is built in the shape of a cross and crowned by a vast dome. Beneath this, a huge bronze canopy covers the altar. St. Peter's can hold up to 50,000 people. Huge crowds gather outside, in the immense Square of St. Peter, to hear the Pope speak from a balcony.

▲ WHERE IS THE HOLY CITY OF THE HINDUS?

The Hindus' holy city is Varanasi in India. It stands on the River Ganges in the north central state of Uttar Pradesh. It used to be known as Benares.

Varanasi stands on the left bank of the Ganges, in southeast Uttar Pradesh. To Hindus, this city is one of the holiest places on earth. They believe that worshipping their gods at the river brings a special reward. They also believe that dying there will free them from having to be reborn.

More than a million pilgrims go to Varanasi each year from all over India. They wade into the Ganges at the *ghats*, bathing places where steps lead down to the river.

Pilgrims worship in the city's 1,500 temples. Rows of temples, shrines and palaces rise from the bank of the Ganges. Many have beautifully carved decorations. For Hindus the most important building is the Golden Temple, which honors the god Shiva.

▼ WHERE DO CHRISTIANS MAKE PILGRIMAGE?

A pilgrimage is a journey to a holy place, or shrine. The greatest Christian center of pilgrimage is at Lourdes in southwest France.

Lourdes is a town in the region of Hautes-Pyrénées, near the Pyrenees Mountains. Roman Catholics believe that the Virgin Mary appeared there several times in 1858 to a peasant girl. Fourteen-year-old Bernadette Soubirous said she had seen these visions in a cave at nearby Massabielle. In 1862, the Roman Catholic Church declared it believed the visions had taken place.

More than two million pilgrims from all over the world now visit Lourdes each year. Many are very ill. They hope to be cured by spring waters in the cave which are said to have healing powers.

In 1958 an immense underground church, the Basilica of St. Pious X, was built at Lourdes. It can hold up to 20,000 pilgrims at once, and is the second largest Roman Catholic church in the world.

▼ WHERE IS THE BIGGEST STATUE OF BUDDHA?

The largest statue of Buddha stands near the town of Bamian. This is in the north of Afghanistan, a country of west-central Asia between Iran, Pakistan and the USSR.

Bamian lies in the valley of the Bamian River. This is about 8,530 feet above sea level, in the Hindu Kush Mountains west of the Himalayas.

About 14 centuries ago, Buddhist monks cut hundreds of cave dwellings into the soft cliffs lining the valley north of the town.

Bamian became famous as a center of Buddhist worship and art. Sculptors carved two huge statues of Buddha out of the solid rock. They added on ridges of mortar to look like the folds in clothing. The larger figure stands 175 feet high and once gleamed with jewels and gold.

Also near Bamian are the remains of the world's longest statue, over 985 feet long. Built of rubble covered with plaster, it shows Buddha lying down.

▲ WHICH CITIES ARE BUILT ON CANALS?

Venice and Amsterdam are canal cities. Venice, shown here, is built on islands divided by canals. Amsterdam stands on land below sea level and is drained by canals.

Venice lies in northeast Italy, in the Adriatic Sea. It was founded in AD 452 by people escaping from barbarian invaders of mainland Italy. Venice later became a rich trading city, and many great palaces and churches were built on its islands.

Venice has more than 1,500 canals crossed by over 400 bridges. Many of the houses stand on wooden posts sunk in the mud. The islands are now sinking, and many of the buildings have been damaged by rising water.

Amsterdam is the capital of the Netherlands. It was founded in about 1275 and became a great trading center in the 1500s. The city stands on low-lying land and is drained by a network of canals shaped something like a spider's web.

▼ WHERE ARE THE LOW COUNTRIES?

The Low Countries are the Netherlands, Belgium and Luxembourg. They lie in northwest Europe and are bordered by France, West Germany and the North Sea. They are known as the Low Countries because much of their land is low-lying.

The Netherlands is the most low-lying of the Low Countries (its name means "Low Lands"). About 40 percent of its land has been reclaimed from the sea. These areas, known as polders, are below sea level and are surrounded by dikes. Machines continuously pump water out of the polders into drainage ditches and canals. Windmills were once used for this.

Belgium lies south of the Netherlands. Its northern region, Flanders, consists of low-lying polders. But the Ardennes, in the southeast, is a hilly forested region. Luxembourg, to the southeast of Belgium, also has hills and lowland. It is one of the smallest countries in Europe.

▶ WHERE IS THE BLACK FOREST?

The Black Forest is a mountainous region in the south of West Germany. It borders the River Rhine, in the province of Baden-Württemberg.

The Black Forest measures about 100 miles from north to south, and varies between 10 and 25 miles in width. The northern part is mostly a sandstone plateau, and there are granite mountains in the south. The highest point is a peak called the Feldberg. This is 4,920 feet above sea level. The River Danube begins in the Black Forest.

Dark forests of firs and spruces cover the mountains in much of the north. These give the Black Forest its name. Oak and beech forests grow on the

slopes, and grapes and other fruits are grown in the valleys.

Tourists visit the Black Forest for hiking holidays. Many stay at local towns such as Baden-Baden, which have mineral springs.

▼ WHERE IS VERSAILLES?

The city of Versailles is in northern France, a few miles southwest of Paris. Nearby stands the palace of Versailles.

The palace of Versailles was built for King Louis XIV in the late 1600s. Before then, Versailles consisted of a few houses in woods where the French kings went hunting.

The palace is more than 2,625 feet long and has hundreds of rooms. Many of the rooms are splendidly

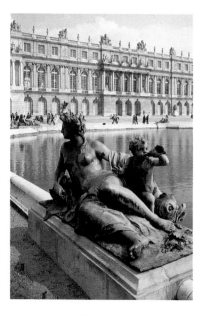

decorated. The palace overlooks a huge park with lawns and walks laid out in patterns. There are pools and fountains also, and a canal which is one mile long. Also in the park are two smaller palaces called the Grand Trianon and the Petit Trianon.

Several historic events have taken place at Versailles. A meeting of the French parliament there in 1789 led to the start of the French Revolution. In 1919 the Treaty of Versailles, marking the end of World War I, was signed in the palace.

▼ WHERE ARE GOTHIC CATHEDRALS FOUND?

Many cathedrals were built in the Gothic style in Europe between the 1100s and 1400s. The earliest and finest of these are found in northern Europe.

Gothic cathedrals are tall, graceful buildings with pointed arches and slender pillars. Many have brightly colored stained-glass windows. Early critics of this style of architecture named it after barbarian tribes called the Goths.

The earliest Gothic cathedral was built at Sens in northern France. One of the most splendid is Chartres Cathedral (shown here), also in northern France. This was built between 1194 and 1225.

Chartres Cathedral has the widest nave and the tallest spires in France. Its great stained-glass windows show saints and scenes from the Bible. It also has a maze through which worshippers used to crawl on their knees. The cathedral stands on a hill and its tall twin spires can be seen from a great distance.

▼ WHERE IS TROOPING THE COLOR HELD?

Trooping the Color is a ceremony held in London. It takes place each year on the British monarch's official birthday.

Trooping the Color takes place on Horse Guards Parade on a Saturday early in June. The ceremony involves carrying a regimental flag, or Color, between formations of soldiers. Each year a different regiment's flag is trooped, but the regiment is always one of those in the Household Brigade of Guards. These form the sovereign's personal bodyguard, and the sovereign acts as each regiment's colonel-in-chief.

First, the guards line up along two sides of a square. Then the brigade's massed bands form up. A sergeant with two guardsmen bears the Color to the front of the parade. All three salute the sovereign, who then inspects the parade. Trooping the Color follows. In the past, colors were carried on to the battlefield in wartime to identify each regiment.

89

▼ WHERE IS THE PONTE VECCHIO?

Ponte Vecchio **means "old bridge." The Ponte Vecchio is the oldest and most famous bridge in Florence, the capital of Tuscany in Italy.**

The Ponte Vecchio stands on the River Arno which flows through the city. The bridge is many hundreds of years old and was rebuilt in 1345.

Unlike modern bridges, the Ponte Vecchio has a row of buildings containing shops along each side of it. The backs of these goldsmiths' and jewelers' shops jut over the river on wooden brackets. Instead of shops, three open arches flank each side of the middle of the bridge.

Long ago, a corridor was built on top of the bridge to connect the Pitti Palace south of the river with the Uffizi Palace which stands on the north bank. The corridor was damaged in World War II. The Ponte Vecchio was the only bridge in Florence which was not destroyed in World War II.

▲ WHERE IS THE ESCORIAL?

The Escorial stands in central Spain, about 31 miles northwest of Madrid. It is a huge building with several parts, including a church, a convent, a palace and a royal burial place.

The Escorial rises among the Guadarrama Mountains as a great granite rectangle with towers at the corners. It has 86 stairs, 1,200 doors and over 2,600 windows. There are also 1,600 paintings and a big library.

The Escorial is one of the finest Spanish buildings put up in the late 1500s. From the outside it looks grim, but there are splendid rooms and courtyards inside. The best features include a great domed church and a cloister with a fountain.

King Philip II had the Escorial built as somewhere to live, pray and study quietly, and as a royal tomb. Philip II and some of Spain's later kings were buried under the church.

▼ WHERE IS THE LEANING TOWER?

The Leaning Tower is in Pisa, a city of Tuscany in west-central Italy. Some people rank the tower as one of the wonders of the modern world. It began tilting hundreds of years ago.

The Leaning Tower is the bell tower of the cathedral of Pisa. It stands 178 feet high and measures 52 feet around the base. The top of the tower is over 13 feet out of line with the base. It leans so far that it looks as if it will topple over at any moment.

Construction of the tower began in 1174 but it remained incomplete until 1350. Before it was half finished, the ground sank under its weight and the tower started tilting. Since 1918, yearly measurements have been made. They show that the lean is increasing.

The tower is made of marble and built in a style known as Romanesque. Rows of rounded arches resting on columns surround its eight floors. People can climb to the top of the tower by a stairway inside.

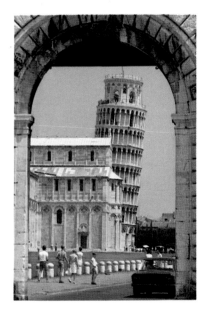

▼ WHERE IS THE ALHAMBRA?

The Alhambra is a famous old palace fortress at Granada, a city in southern Spain. It was built by the Moors, a Muslim people who ruled Spain in the Middle Ages.

The Alhambra stands on a hill below the Sierra Nevada mountains and overlooking Granada. The Moorish kings of Granada built the Alhambra between 1248 and 1354. It was the last Moorish stronghold in Europe. Its name is Arabic for "the red" and probably comes from the red bricks of its outer wall.

The wall and its 13 towers enclose the palace and gardens. The palace is small but lovely. Slim columns, marble floors, tiled walls and lace-like moldings on walls and ceilings adorn its chambers and courtyards. Moldings show words from the *Koran*, the holy book of Islam, delicately done in Arabic script. Fountains play from pools in the courts and gardens. Palms and other sub-tropical plants grow there.

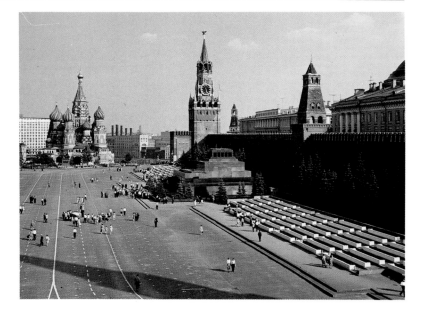

▲ WHERE IS THE KREMLIN?

The Kremlin is the old center of Moscow, the capital of the Soviet Union. Its walls and towers rise from a hill on the left bank of the River Moskva.

The name *kremlin* comes from a Russian word meaning "fortress." The Kremlin is a group of buildings surrounded by high walls crowned with 20 towers and entered through six gates. The walls form a triangle with sides that total 1.5 miles in length.

The first walls were built of wood, eight centuries ago. Today's great walls date from the late 1400s. Inside, splendid cathedrals with gilded domes face a central square. Here, too, is the Great Kremlin Palace.

The Kremlin was once the Russian emperor's Moscow home. Now the Soviet government and the Communist Party hold meetings there. The Kremlin has many art treasures and since 1955 it has been a national museum.

▲ WHERE IS RED SQUARE?

Red Square lies just outside the northeast wall of the Kremlin in Moscow. Its name comes from an old Russian word that means "red" or "beautiful."

Red Square is an immensely broad, paved open-space about 1,300 feet long. It forms the most famous of the so-called central squares in the heart of Moscow.

Red Square is best-known for the huge parades that pass through to celebrate May Day and the anniversary of the Russian Revolution. Thousands of people march past in processions that last several hours. Russian leaders watch from above the Lenin Mausoleum.

The photograph shows Red Square and the wall of the Kremlin. In front of the Kremlin is Lenin's tomb. Every day, Russians visit the tomb to pay homage to Lenin, the founder of the modern Soviet Union. In the background is St. Basil's Cathedral, with its cluster of colorful domes.

91

◄ WHICH GREAT CITY HAS HAD FOUR NAMES?

Istanbul, in northwest Turkey, was once called Constantinople or New Rome. Earlier still, people called it Byzantium.

Istanbul is Turkey's largest city and seaport, and one of the world's oldest cities. Part stands in Europe and part in Asia. Separating both parts lies a narrow strait called the Bosporus, which links the Black Sea with the Mediterranean.

According to legend, a Greek called Byzas founded Byzantium on the European side of the Bosporus in 657 BC. In AD 330, the Emperor Constantine made Byzantium the capital of the Eastern Roman Empire. Constantine enlarged it and renamed it New Rome, but it became known as Constantinople (from Greek words meaning "Constantine's city").

In 1453, the Turks captured Constantinople. It became known as *Istanbul*, a Turkish version of Greek words meaning "in the city."

◄ WHERE IS THE KRAK DES CHEVALIERS?

This huge medieval castle stands in the mountains of Western Syria. It was one of the greatest castles to be built in the 12th century.

The Krak des Chevaliers, or Krak of the Knights, began as a fort called the *Hisn el-Akrad*: "Castle of the Kurds." Christian Crusaders seized it from their Muslim enemies in 1109, and then rebuilt it. Using forts in the East as a model, they made an outer "curtain wall" protecting an inner stronghold, with tall linked towers.

The Krak's defenders could stand at slits in the top of the outer wall and its towers to fire arrows or hurl stones at attackers below. From holes in the wall, they could pour hot pitch onto their enemies' heads.

The Krak was one of the most important castles for defending the borders of the states set up by Christian Crusaders. The Knights Hospitallers held it from 1142 to 1271.

◄ WHICH ARE THE RICHEST COUNTRIES IN THE WORLD?

This depends on how you measure a country's wealth. One way is to work out the wealth of each person in a country, supposing that all the wealth were shared out equally. Measured in this way, the wealthiest countries are a few Arab states in southwest Asia.

The richest Arab states are those with small populations but huge supplies of valuable oil. Profits from the sale of oil have helped such states to improve their standard of living. Most of these states are on the Persian Gulf.

The states with the most wealth per head of population in the early 1980s were the United Arab Emirates. Altogether these had fewer than one million people. If all wealth were shared equally among their people, in 1980 each person would have had $30,070.

The photograph shows an oil rig on the Persian Gulf. Excess gas from the oil is being burned off.

▶ WHERE IS ISFAHAN?

Isfahan stands in western Iran, about 248 miles south of the capital, Tehran. Isfahan is an old city with some splendid buildings.

Isfahan's name may come from an Old Persian word for "army camp," but the city grew up as a trading center set in rich farmlands watered by the Zaindeh ("life-giving") river.

In 1598, Shah Abbas the Great made Isfahan the Persian capital. The Shah rebuilt it as one of the world's largest and loveliest cities. He added the huge Royal Square, palaces, public buildings and mosques. Many of these still exist.

The photograph shows the Masjid-i-Shah (Royal Mosque) at the south end of the Royal Square. The mosque's dome is covered in blue enamelled tiles that shine brilliantly in sunlight.

West of the Royal Square stands the Ali Qapu ("lofty gate"). This archway, crowned by a high covered balcony, leads into the gardens of the old royal palace.

▶ WHERE IS BANGLADESH?

Bangladesh is a small Muslim country in tropical Asia. It is almost surrounded by eastern India which lies along its western, northern and eastern borders. On its southern boundary is the Bay of Bengal.

The name Bangladesh means "Bengal nation." Bangladesh stands on the Bay of Bengal where the great delta of the Ganges and Brahmaputra rivers juts into the sea.

Bangladesh is less than two-thirds the size of the United Kingdom, yet its population is almost twice as big. Farmers grow rice and other tropical crops on rich soil in the hot river plain and delta. Bangladesh produces most of the world's jute, a plant that yields fibers used for making sacks and wrappings.

When India and Pakistan became independent in 1947, Bangladesh became part of Pakistan, and was known as East Pakistan. After a war in 1971, Bangladesh became a separate country.

▶ WHERE IS THE GATEWAY OF INDIA?

The Gateway of India is a great archway on the waterfront of the port of Bombay, in western India.

India's British rulers built the Gateway to mark a royal event. This was a visit to India in 1911 by King George V and Queen Mary. At that time, the British sovereign was also the emperor of India.

Its architect built the Gateway of India as a kind of mighty triumphal arch, a type of building made famous long before by the Romans. But he designed its arches and towers in the Indian Gujarat style of the 16th century.

It seemed fitting to erect the Gateway of India in Bombay. Under the British, this port on the Arabian Sea had grown into the main port of arrival for ships sailing to India from Europe and North America. Its deep-water harbor, protected by islands, has helped to make Bombay one of Asia's great cities.

93

◄ WHERE IS THE TAJ MAHAL?

This beautiful tomb stands in a garden outside the city of Agra, in north central India. The Mogul Emperor Shah Jahan had the Taj Mahal built in memory of his favorite wife, Mumtaz Mahal.

Shah Jahan ordered work to begin after his wife died in 1631. Some 20,000 workmen spent more than 20 years making the tomb and laying out its garden.

The bodies of Shah Jahan and his wife lie in a vault below a tall, eight-sided building of white marble, pierced by immense arches and crowned by a delicate dome. This mausoleum stands on the middle of a great square marble platform. Four tall prayer towers, or minarets, rise from its corners.

Two identical mosques of marble and red sandstone flank the mausoleum. The group of buildings stands in a walled garden, where a long pool reflects the domed mausoleum.

► WHERE IS THE GOLDEN PAGODA?

The Golden Pagoda is a great Buddhist shrine which overlooks Rangoon, the capital of Burma. Its proper name is the Shwe Dagon Pagoda.

The Shwe Dagon Pagoda rises 367 feet from the top of a hill in northern Rangoon. It is built of brick and shaped like an immense cone. Such cone- or bell-shaped pagodas are also called *stupas*. A layer of pure beaten gold covers the shrine from top to bottom. At its base stand much smaller, more delicate stupas.

The main stupa covers a chamber which is believed to hold eight of the Buddha's hairs. For Buddhists, these relics make the shrine especially holy.

At Buddhist festivals, people from all over Burma make pilgrimages to the Shwe Dagon Pagoda. They meditate and worship on the great terrace surrounding the foot of the Golden Pagoda.

◄ WHERE ARE ELEPHANTS USED AS WORKING ANIMALS?

In Asian countries such as India and Burma, elephants are used as beasts of burden.

Trained elephants work mostly at shifting trees that have been felled in forests. They can use their trunks and tusks to lift small logs. Full-grown elephants are strong enough to pull logs weighing up to two tons. Young elephants are used mostly for uprooting and clearing away undergrowth.

Each elephant obeys orders given by its trainer, or *mahout*, who sits on its back. Well-trained elephants will kneel, stand and walk, and obey other simple commands.

Unlike horses, and other domesticated animals, elephants do not breed readily in captivity. For this reason, each elephant is captured in the wild and then trained for work. Wild elephants are now in danger of dying out in Asia, so the days of the working elephant might be numbered too.

▶ WHICH CITY HAS "KLONGS"?

Klongs **are the canals of Bangkok, the capital city of Thailand in Southeast Asia.**

Klongs were once so important to life in Bangkok that Western visitors called it "the Venice of the East." Throughout the 19th century, most people lived in houses built on stilts driven down into the mud at the edges of canals and the Chao Phraya, the river flowing through Bangkok.

Bangkok had no important roads until 1864, when workers built the Royal Road to connect the king's palace to the buildings downstream where foreign officials lived. By 1910 most people had left the waterside and settled in homes near newly built roads.

Many Thais still live by the klongs and travel on them. Much of the food and timber from Thailand's farms and forests still reaches Bangkok by canal. A network of canals connects the city to three rivers of the central plain.

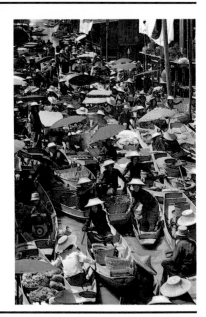

◀ WHICH ASIAN CITY AND COUNTRY SHARE THE SAME NAME?

Singapore city is the capital of a tiny South-East Asian country, also called Singapore. The name means "city of the lions." Singapore is one of the richest countries in Asia.

The republic of Singapore is a group of small islands just south of the Malay Peninsula. Singapore Island, the largest island, is about the same size as Chicago.

Singapore city stands in the south of Singapore island. It was a small fishing village backed by jungle when British colonists arrived in the 1820s. They made the fine natural harbor into a great port at a crossroads of trade between East and West.

Today, Singapore city is one of Asia's chief trading and banking centres. There are modern factories, high-rise flats, and skyscraper office blocks. Most of Singapore's population lives and works in the capital.

▶ WHAT ARE CHINESE PAGODAS?

Chinese pagodas are towers with a number of floors, each with its own roof. Pagodas serve as Buddhist shrines.

Pagodas often have eight sides and up to 12 floors. They may be made of wood, brick or stone. Each story has a roof of colored, glazed tiles. This curves up at the eaves.

Pagodas are a mixture of Chinese and Indian building styles. The shape of pagodas came from old Chinese watch-towers, which were also built up in stages. But the idea of towers as shrines came from Indian towers and domes called *stupas*. Like stupas, many Chinese pagodas are crowned by what looks like several umbrellas, one above the other. This was a sign that a building had been raised in honour of a royal person.

As long ago as AD 516, the Chinese built a wooden pagoda about 328 feet tall. Most early wooden towers fell down long ago. Some survive in Japan, where this building style was copied.

▲ WHERE IS TAKING TEA A CEREMONY?

The tea ceremony is a traditional custom in Japan. The Japanese call it *cha-no-yu*, which means simply "hot water tea."

The Japanese tea ceremony is a formal occasion and is carried out according to precise rules. The ceremony is linked to the Zen Buddhist belief that we should find beauty in the ordinary things of daily life.

Tea ceremonies take place in simple, quiet surroundings, often in a special room set aside for the purpose. When the guests have assembled, the hostess begins to prepare the tea with plain, simple utensils. The tea is made by stirring crushed leaves into hot water, and is served in a bowl. After each guest has drunk from the bowl, it is rinsed and filled for the next person.

The atmosphere during the ceremony is serene and peaceful. The guests sit opposite their hostess and talk only of what is taking place during the ritual.

▼ WHICH IS THE WORLD'S BIGGEST CITY?

Tokyo, Peking and Mexico City are all huge. In the early 1980s the city with the most people was Tokyo, the capital of Japan.

Tokyo lies on Tokyo Bay on the east coast of Honshu, the largest Japanese island. It was founded in the 1400s, when it was called Edo.

In 1980, Greater Tokyo had more than 11,350,000 people. But Tokyo and nearby cities had grown so large that they merged. Tokyo and Yokohama, together with their suburbs, form the huge Keihin Metropolitan Area. By the early 1980s, its population was about 28 million. Belgium, in contrast, has ten times the area but a population of only about ten million. Yet Belgium is considered to be a densely populated country.

Tokyo's industries produce metals, chemicals, machinery, textiles and electronic equipment. The city has more than 200 colleges and universities. Yokohama serves as its port.

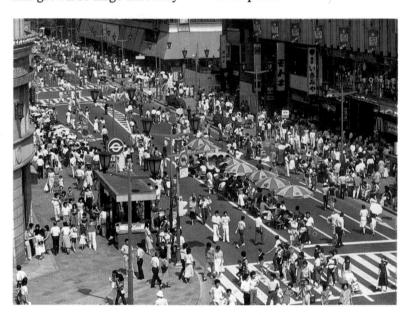

▲ WHERE IS GINZA?

Ginza Street, in the Ginza district of Tokyo, is the Japanese capital's great shopping center. *Ginza* is a Japanese word for silver articles, which craftsmen made there.

Ginza Street runs from northeast to southwest through a part of Tokyo between the Imperial Palace and Tokyo Bay. Nihonbashi Street, at the northern end of Ginza Street, has Tokyo's finest department stores. At night the whole street is brightly illuminated.

The Ginza lies close to other important parts of Tokyo. The Emperor lives in the Imperial Palace, nearby. The nearby Marunouchi district is Japan's center of big business. Government offices and an amusement center are also not far away.

Much of this area is in the old heart of Tokyo. Fires often burned down the city's old wooden buildings. After fire destroyed the Ginza in 1872, it was rebuilt in brick from plans drawn up by a British engineer.

▼ WHERE IS THE FORBIDDEN CITY?

The Forbidden City is an old royal part of the Chinese capital Beijing (Peking). Ordinary people were once forbidden to enter buildings in this part of the city.

The Forbidden City (shown here) stands in the center of the northern half of Beijing. The Forbidden City forms a large square surrounded by a moat 2 miles long, and a high brick wall.

A gate in the wall leads inside to a number of buildings once used by the Chinese emperors. Imposing throne-halls, roofed with gold tiles, stand on white marble terraces. There are several other palace buildings and courts. These palaces now serve as museums for Chinese works of art. Ordinary Chinese people may now visit this part of Beijing.

Another "forbidden city" is Lhasa in Tibet. Lhasa was a religious center for Tibetan Buddhists, and the Tibetans once refused to let Europeans enter the city.

▲ WHICH COUNTRY HAS THE LARGEST POPULATION?

The country with the largest population is the People's Republic of China. By the mid-1980s China had more than 1,000 million inhabitants.

China is the world's third largest country after the USSR and Canada, but it has the largest population. One person out of every four on earth lives in China.

Most Chinese people live in cities and on farms in the valleys and plains of eastern China. Few live in the deserts of the north or the vast mountainous areas of the west.

The Chinese population has grown fast with improved methods of farming and health care. The Chinese are worried by the rate of increase. They fear that there will not be enough food for future generations. The government is trying to reduce the population by discouraging parents from having more than one child.

▼ WHERE DO PEOPLE MAKE GARDENS FROM STONES?

In Japan, gardens are a form of art. Stones, sand and pools of water are carefully arranged to create a landscape of peace and quiet beauty.

The design of Japanese gardens has been influenced by Zen Buddhism. In this school of religion, beauty is seen in simplicity. Long ago, Japanese Zen priests gave special names to rocks set in certain positions. For instance, a garden might include a flat "worshipping" stone and a tall, solitary "guardian" stone.

There are two main types of Japanese garden. One is the *hira-niwa* ("level ground"), which has specially arranged rocks set in a bed of raked white sand. The other is the *tsuki-yama* ("artificial hills"), which has hills and ponds. Rocks are chosen to look like distant peaks and mountain slopes. Japanese gardens also have evergreen shrubs and trees, but few flowering plants. The Japanese also make tiny stone gardens in trays. These are called *bon-seki*.

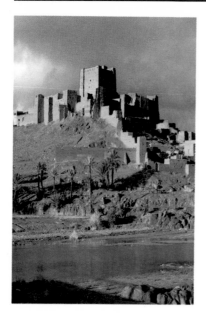

▲ WHERE CAN YOU SEE A CASBAH?

▲ WHERE ARE SOUKS FOUND?

▼ WHERE IS TIMBUKTU?

Casbahs are fortresses. They were built by tribal chieftains in North African countries such as Morocco and Algeria.

Casbahs are imposing citadels with tall square towers and high walls. Within the walls are living quarters, storerooms and courtyards.

Many casbahs were built in the Atlas Mountains by Berbers, the original inhabitants of North Africa. Berber chieftains ruled from casbahs much as the European barons ruled from their castles in medieval times.

Fortified walled villages are also found close to casbahs at oases on the edge of the Sahara. They were built of mud, and provided protection against enemy tribes and invaders from the desert.

Famous casbahs include the residence of the dey, or governor, of Algiers, and the casbah at Telouet in the High Atlas. A great casbah at Tifoultout in southern Morocco has been preserved and turned into a hotel.

Souks are Arab markets. North African towns have permanent souks, but in country areas there are weekly market days.

In North African cities, shops and stalls are set in old, narrow streets, with closely packed houses. Many houses have a ground-floor workshop, and a shop that opens on to the street. Such shops sell goods that you can see being made in the workshops behind. You can buy anything in a souk, from handmade brassware or carpets to honeyed pastries and spiced roasted meats. Merchants may offer their customers a cup of coffee or a glass of tea while they bargain over an article's price.

Some of Morocco's farming centers are named after their weekly market day. Thus Souk-el-Khemis means "Thursday Market." Weekly markets often take place at deserted spots in the country. Merchants, cobblers, blacksmiths, barbers and villagers flock in on foot, or by bus, to buy and sell.

Timbuktu is an ancient African town just south of the Sahara Desert. It was once one of the biggest, richest and most famous cities in Africa.

Timbuktu is near the Niger River, in the center of the republic of Mali. Here the desert meets more fertile land to the south. Timbuktu grew up where farmers met nomads to trade. Its name means "place of Buktu." According to legend, a slave called Buktu was left there to mind her nomad owners' possessions.

In the Middle Ages, Timbuktu became famous for gold, salt and slaves. Camel caravans stopped there on long trading treks across the Sahara. By the 1500s, Timbuktu was also a great center of Muslim learning and had a million inhabitants.

Hundreds of years of warfare followed. Timbuktu was a ruined town when the French conquered it in 1893. Today Timbuktu is a small town of flat-roofed homes built of sun-dried mud brick. It trades mainly in salt.

98

► WHERE IS THE LARGEST AFRICAN NATIONAL PARK?

The largest African national park is the Tsavo National Park in the East African country of Kenya. The park is one of the world's richest wildlife reserves.

Tsavo National Park lies in southern Kenya. The park is slightly larger than the country of Israel. It consists of dry open plains covered with tropical grasses and scrub. Strips of woodland grow along river banks. There are also long, rocky ridges and lonely outcrops of rock.

Visitors come from all over the world to see the park's many wild mammals and birds. Lions, leopards and cheetahs hunt antelope such as gerenuk, eland and waterbuck. Giraffes, black rhinos and herds of elephants range through the scrub.

There are hundreds of species of birds. They include great eagles, tiny sunbirds, stately herons, colorful weavers and starlings. There are also eight kinds of hornbill. These are birds with huge beaks.

▲ WHERE DO PEOPLE GO ON SAFARI?

"Safari" comes from an Arabic word that means "of a trip." Safaris are trips made to hunt or watch wild animals, especially in East Africa.

Until recently, hunters used to go on safari to kill the big game that teemed in what are now Kenya, Uganda and Tanzania. White and black hunters and farmers killed so many animals that some species became rare. Many animals now live in protected national parks or game reserves.

The most famous parks include Kenya's Tsavo National Park and Tanzania's Serengeti National Park and Ngorongoro Crater. Here people go on safari with cameras, not guns. They watch and film the wildlife instead of shooting to kill. Many visitors arrive by bus or plane.

Although some rare kinds of animals are now protected by law, many are still killed by poachers. African elephants, for example, are slaughtered for their valuable ivory tusks.

▲ WHERE ARE THE OLDEST CHURCHES IN AFRICA?

Africa's oldest surviving churches stand in northeast Africa, in the ancient African country of Ethiopia.

Christianity reached what is now Ethiopia in the fourth century AD, but the best-known Ethiopian churches are about eight centuries old. Eleven of them stand at the small town of Lalibela in the mountains of north central Ethiopia. Workers carved the churches out of solid rock.

The largest church is the Medhane Alem ("The Savior of the World"). It measures 108 feet in length and 36 feet in height. Its roof is level with the top of the rest of the rock from which it was carved. A deep trench separates the church from the natural rock.

Ethiopian builders might have learned this way of building from Indian architects. Legend has it that King Lalibela had most of these churches built between 1181 and 1221.

▼ WHERE ARE OASES FOUND?

Oases are moist places in deserts. Here, plants grow and there may be enough food and water for passers-by or people making a permanent home.

Oases are found in the Sahara, Gobi and other great deserts of the world. They occur wherever the ground holds a good supply of fresh water.

In North American deserts, oases are often found in valleys where water soaks into the soil after running off mountains. In the Sahara Desert there are oases where springs bubble up, or where underground streams or layers of water lie high enough to be reached by digging a well.

Oases vary in size and shape. Some are just a clump of trees around a small spring. The Nile Valley in Egypt is a narrow oasis hundreds of miles long. The River Nile waters crops which are planted along its banks. This huge oasis grows enough food for millions of people. Tropical oases produce crops such as dates, rice and wheat.

▼ WHERE IS THE LONGEST BIG-SHIP CANAL?

The longest canal able to take large seagoing ships is the Suez Canal. This passes through Egypt to connect the Mediterranean Sea and the Red Sea.

The Suez Canal measures 100 miles. It joins the cities of Port Said in the north and Suez in the south. Between the cities it crosses the Isthmus of Suez, a narrow neck of land that links Africa to Asia. The canal passes through several lakes, including the Bitter Lakes, on the way.

The French engineer Ferdinand de Lesseps had the canal built between 1859 and 1869. It shortened a voyage from Britain to India by 3,472 miles.

At first, the waterway was only 26 feet deep and 72 feet wide at the bottom. As larger ships began to be built, the canal became too shallow and narrow. It is now being widened and deepened so that it can take ships designed for loads of 225,000 tons.

▲ WHERE WAS THE BENIN EMPIRE?

Benin was an old kingdom in West Africa. Its center lay in what is now southwest Nigeria, not the modern country of Benin.

The kingdom of Benin gave its name to the forested coastland of what are now eastern Ghana, Togo, Benin and Nigeria. Benin reached its peak of power and prosperity between the 1300s and 1600s.

By the late 1400s the *oba*, or king, of Benin controlled an empire stretching for hundreds of miles with the help of his well trained army. The capital was Benin City. About 80,000 people lived there in neat rows of huts surrounded by a wall and a moat. Many were skilled craftspeople. Benin metalworkers cast fine heads in bronze and brass, like the one shown here.

Benin City became an important center of trade between inland Negroes and Europeans on the coast. But by the late 1800s wars and slave-raiding had made Benin poor and weak.

▼ WHERE IS GREAT ZIMBABWE?

Great Zimbabwe is a ruined stone city in southern Africa. Its name means "Houses of Stone."

Great Zimbabwe stands in a valley among rocky hills in southeast Zimbabwe. The roofless ruins consist of granite blocks piled up without the use of cement. There are three groups of buildings, known as the Acropolis, Valley Ruins and Temple. The Acropolis has massive walls and a maze

▶ WHERE ARE THE VICTORIA FALLS?

The Victoria Falls are a great waterfall in south central Africa. They stand on the Zambezi River where it flows between Zambia and Zimbabwe.

The Zambezi is about a mile wide at the falls. Here the river plunges over a cliff of hard volcanic rock up to 354 feet in depth. Below the falls the river flows on through a deep, narrow gorge worn by the falling water. This gorge is 40 miles long. In all Africa, only the Boyoma Falls on the Zaire River carry more water.

As the water crashes down, it hurls a cloud of spray and mist high in the air. People can see it from miles away. Local Africans called the falls *Mosi-oa-tunya* ("The Smoke that

of corridors and curved stairs. The Valley Ruins are smaller buildings. The Temple's high walls enclose a mysterious solid tower.

Archaeologists think that Bantu-speaking Shona Negroes built Great Zimbabwe between AD 1200 and 1450. The Shonas' rulers grew rich by trading in gold. These priest-kings probably lived in Great Zimbabwe. Its high walls hid them from the gaze of the people, for Shonas worshipped their priest-kings almost as if they were gods.

Thunders"). The Scottish explorer David Livingstone was the first European to see the falls, in 1855. He named them after Queen Victoria of Britain.

▼ WHERE DO ZULUS LIVE?

Zulus are a Bantu-speaking Negro people who live in part of eastern South Africa. They were once famous as warriors.

More than five million Zulus live in the northeast of the South African province of Natal. Their homeland is usually called Zululand, but the South African government uses the name KwaZulu ("the Zulu nation") for the Zulus' own territory.

Zulus are strongly built people. They live in *kraals*, villages with cattle pens surrounded by huts. Young men once formed regiments called *impis*. These worked and fought for the Zulu king.

In the early 1800s the Zulus were a small, local tribe. Then their chief, Shaka, built up a powerful army of warriors armed with light stabbing spears called *assegais*. His troops terrified neighboring tribes and mastered all of what is now Natal. In 1879 the Zulus, led by their king, Cetewayo, fought British troops in the Zulu War. The Zulus were defeated.

◄ WHERE IS THE STATUE OF LIBERTY?

This immense statue rises from Liberty Island in New York Harbor. It is one of the world's tallest statues.

The statue shows a woman wearing a robe and holding a huge burning torch aloft in her right hand. The left hand holds a tablet bearing the date of the American Declaration of Independence (1776).

The figure is made of thin copper sheets fixed over an iron framework held up by steel columns. It weighs over 200 tons and rises 150 feet from an immense pedestal which is 154 feet high.

People can climb up inside the statue by means of a lift and a spiral stairway. At night the torch shines with a powerful light and the statue is floodlit.

The French sculptor Frédéric-Auguste Bartholdi designed the statue. It was made in France as a gift from France to the United States. The statue arrived there by ship in separate pieces in 1885.

◄ WHERE IS MANHATTAN?

Manhattan is an island in New York State. It forms the heart of New York city.

Manhattan Island is a narrow island about 13 miles long and 2 miles wide. It lies east of the Hudson River, and west of the East River, with New York Bay to the south and the Harlem River to the north.

The island is one of the world's great business and cultural centers. Some of the world's tallest skyscraper buildings tower over the south of Manhattan. Manhattan also has the famous theaters of Broadway, New York's Stock Exchange and the smart stores of Fifth Avenue. Its best-known landmarks include the United Nations Building, the American Museum of Natural History, the Metropolitan Museum of Art and Central Park.

Indians called the island *Man-a-hat-ta*, meaning "Heavenly Land." Dutch colonists bought it from them in 1626 for a handful of cloth and trinkets.

◄ WHERE IS THE WHITE HOUSE?

The White House stands in Washington, DC, the capital of the United States. It is the official residence of the president of the country.

The White House stands on Pennsylvania Avenue amid lawns, trees and flowerbeds. Each year more than a million people visit parts of the house open to the public.

The imposing main building has a great porch like the front of an ancient temple. Inside are richly decorated state rooms. The president lives in rooms above.

Long, low galleries jut out to the east and west. Beyond lie the West and East wings. The West Wing contains offices where the president and his staff work. Other staff work in the East Wing.

Construction of the White House began in 1792. It was rebuilt and enlarged after the British burned it in 1814. The name first came from its white limestone walls, which were later painted white to hide the fire damage.

▶ WHERE IS CAPE CANAVERAL?

Cape Canaveral is a low sandy cape in the southeast United States. It is the main launch site for American spacecraft and long-range missiles.

Cape Canaveral stands on the east coast of Florida. Its John F. Kennedy Space Center includes the Launch Operations Center of the National Aeronautics and Space Administration (NASA), and the first tracking station of the Atlantic Missile Range.

The first American satellite was launched from Cape Canaveral. In 1969 Neil Armstrong and Edwin Aldrin left the site to become the first people on the moon. Also at the Cape is the start of a missile-testing range that extends across the South Atlantic Ocean.

Visitors to the Cape can see space rockets on exhibit, and the building used for assembling the Apollo spacecraft. The Space Shuttle is also launched at the Cape.

▶ WHERE IS DISNEYLAND?

Disneyland is the world's best-known amusement park. The American film producer Walt Disney built it at Anaheim in California. Disneyland is about 25 miles southeast of Los Angeles.

Some people rate Disneyland as one of the seven wonders of the modern world. Millions of parents and children go there each year from all over the world to enjoy the park's main amusement areas. These are Adventureland, Frontierland, Fantasyland and Tomorrowland.

Visitors enjoy a huge range of attractions. They can bobsled down a miniature Matterhorn mountain, speed through outer space, glide under the ocean by submarine, visit a haunted house, explore the Old Frontier, go on a jungle safari, or be fired on by pirates.

Among the most popular sights are daily parades that include Disney cartoon characters. Many events have been added since Disneyland opened in 1955.

▶ WHERE IS THE LONGEST ARTIFICIAL SEAWAY?

The longest artificial seaway is the St. Lawrence Seaway. This allows oceangoing ships to sail from the Atlantic Ocean to the Great Lakes deep in North America.

The St. Lawrence Seaway runs for about 186 miles along the St. Lawrence River, which flows from Lake Ontario to the Atlantic Ocean. To make the seaway, engineers dredged stretches of river to deepen them. They cut new canals and deepened the old Welland Canal. They also built locks as giant elevators to raise and lower ships from one water level to another.

American and Canadian teams made the seaway, which largely lies between Ontario in Canada and New York State in the United States. It opened in 1959. Big ships using it can sail more than 2,294 miles inland from the Atlantic to a port on Lake Superior. The photograph shows the seaway as it passes through the city of Quebec.

▼ WHERE DID THE OLMECS LIVE?

The Olmecs were Stone Age Indians who lived in Mexico. Their civilization was among the first in Central America.

The Olmec culture flourished about 1100–800 BC in central Mexico and south far into Guatemala. *Olmec* means "rubber people," a name first used for Indians in southeast Mexico, where rubber trees were plentiful.

The Olmecs lacked metal tools, yet carved hard stone with skill. They made stone jaguars, dwarfs and huge human heads. The largest head weighs 15 tons and stands about 8 feet high. Its thick lips and flat nose are unlike those of modern Indians.

The Olmecs made delicate objects, too, such as finely ground and polished stone mirrors. Their carvings suggest that they worshipped a god shown as half jaguar, half human.

The Olmecs had a type of early writing and probably knew a way of measuring the year.

▼ WHERE ARE FOUR AMERICAN PRESIDENTS CARVED OUT OF ROCK?

These immense carvings are cut in the Black Hills of South Dakota, in the midwest United States. They rank among the world's largest sculptures.

The carvings jut from a granite cliff called Mount Rushmore, which is 25 miles southeast of Rapid City. Seen from below, the carvings show the heads of four presidents: George Washington, Thomas Jefferson, Theodore Roosevelt and Abraham Lincoln. The four giant heads are about 59 feet high and can be seen from a distance of 60 miles. The whole group is known as the Mount Rushmore National Memorial.

The American sculptor Gutzon Borglum planned the memorial. Work started in 1927 and lasted into the 1960s. Workmen used drills and dynamite to cut into the cliff face. They had small model faces to guide them as they worked.

▲ WHICH CITY HAS FLOATING GARDENS?

Mexico City, the capital of Mexico, has floating gardens. You can see them at Xochimilco, a southern suburb of Mexico City.

Xochimilco stands on the shores of Lake Xochimilco, and the floating gardens lie on this lake. Xochimilco is an Indian word that means "place of flowers."

Long ago, local Indians grew flowers and vegetables on rafts moored out on the lake. They made these rafts of reeds and twigs woven together and covered with mud. In time, plant roots grew down from the rafts into the bed of the lake.

Today, these floating gardens look like meadows rimmed with flowers and poplar trees. The strips of lake water between the "meadows" resemble canals.

Thousands of tourists visit the gardens each year. Many travel the waterways in canoes decorated with flowers. They punt the canoes along with oars.

▼ WHERE DO NORTH AMERICAN INDIANS LIVE?

In the United States and Canada many Indians live on land set aside for them by the government. These lands are called reserves in Canada and reservations in the United States.

The United States has over 100 reservations and there are more than 2,000 reserves in Canada. Indians do not have to live on these lands, but may avoid paying tax if they do.

Many Indians hunt or farm,

or raise livestock on their tribe's land. Others leave their homes and work in mines, factories or farms elsewhere. Indians living on reserves are often poorer than most North Americans but some tribal lands are rich in minerals or timber.

Reservations and reserves vary greatly in size. The largest reservation is that of the Navaho tribe in Arizona and New Mexico. It is bigger than Portugal in area. The Navaho women in the photograph are weaving patterned rugs on a hand loom.

▼ WHERE ARE TOTEM POLES FOUND?

Totem poles are tall, straight tree trunks carved usually to look like human and animal figures perched one on top of another. They were made by Indians in North America.

Each totem pole showed a totem. A totem is an animal representing a clan, or group of families. In some societies people worship their totem and have rules to forbid killing that kind of animal. Some people also believe that the totem animal is their ancestor.

The tallest totem pole was raised at Alert Bay in Vancouver Island, Canada, in 1973. It is 173 feet high. The area is the home of the Kwakiutl Indians, who were making totem poles hundreds of years ago. This pole's carvings tell the story of the Kwakiutl.

The Kwakiutl used to raise totem poles at a feast called a potlatch, which lasted for several days. To show off his importance, the host of the potlatch would give away vast quantities of his possessions to the guests.

▼ WHERE IS MESA VERDE?

Mesa Verde is a national park in southwestern Colorado, in the United States. It is famous for Indian cliff dwellings.

Mesa Verde means "green table." This name comes from the park's forested hills with flat tops and steep sides like the walls of deep canyons.

Centuries ago, Indians built villages against the undercut walls. The overhanging rock above helped to protect these so-called cliff dwellers from

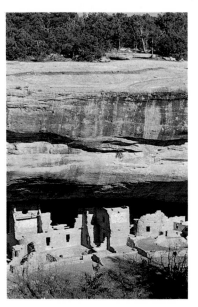

enemy tribes.

Cliff Palace, Long House and Spruce Tree House are names of some of the cliff dwellers' villages. Cliff Palace was the largest. This held up to 400 Indians who lived in 200 rooms built of stone and sun-dried mud. In places, as many as four rooms are built on top of each other. There are also special pit houses called *kivas* where cliff dwellers held religious ceremonies.

Indians probably built most of the cliff-dwellings in the twelfth century AD. Drought drove them out by AD 1300.

105

▼ WHERE IS THE LAND OF FIRE?

"Land of Fire" is the English translation of *Tierra del Fuego*. This is the name of a group of islands at the southern tip of South America.

Tierra del Fuego is a little smaller than Ireland. Most of it is one island, also called Tierra del Fuego. Beyond the Strait of Magellan lies mainland South America.

The name of the islands is misleading. They are often wretchedly wet, windy and cold. Indeed, the name "Land of Fire" comes from bonfires once kept alight by Indians trying to stay warm. The Portuguese explorer Ferdinand Magellan glimpsed these fires in 1520 when he became the first European to sail through the Strait of Magellan.

Today the strait and the western part of the island group belong to Chile. Argentina owns the eastern part of the main island. Ushaia, on the Chilean part of this island, is the world's southernmost city.

► WHERE DO GAUCHOS LIVE?

Gauchos are South American cowboys. They work on cattle ranches on the pampas, the grassy plains of Argentina and Uruguay.

Gauchos were once wandering cowboys who were their own masters. They wore a broad-brimmed hat, colorful scarf, bright shirt, wide silver belt, baggy trousers and high leather boots.

These men were skilled horsemen famed for toughness and bravery. They became expert at catching cows by throwing the *bola*. This was a kind of sling that wrapped itself around the legs of a running cow, tripping it up.

Early gauchos were half Indian, half Spanish. They lived by catching and selling wild cattle. Later, most worked for men who had built up big cattle herds. When farmers fenced in the open range, gauchos lost their old free-roaming way of life. Many became farmhands or soldiers. Today, few of the old-style gauchos are left.

▲ WHICH IS THE HIGHEST CAPITAL CITY?

La Paz, in the South American country of Bolivia, is higher than any other city used as a center of government.

La Paz is about 12,000 feet above sea level. It stands near Lake Titicaca, in the Andes Mountains of western Bolivia. Snow-capped peaks tower high above the city.

More than half a million people live in La Paz. Many work for the government or in factories making products such as flour, beer or leather.

Spanish colonists founded La Paz in 1548. (*Paz* means "Peace.") The town of Sucre is Bolivia's official capital, but La Paz is the center of government. Its population is just over half a million.

► WHERE HAS BRASÍLIA
BEEN BUILT?

**Brasília is a city built in
east-central Brazil. In 1960 it
replaced Rio de Janeiro as
Brazil's center of
government.**

Brasília stands on a plateau
about 600 miles northwest of
Rio de Janeiro. By building a
new capital in the interior,
Brasília's planners hoped to
open up the undeveloped heart
of the country.

Many cities grow gradually,
according to no particular
plan, but Brasília was carefully
designed and built. Lucio
Costa planned its layout to
look like a huge cross. The
Brazilian architect Oscar
Niemeyer designed the main
buildings. Many are tall slabs
of concrete and glass.
Buildings housing the three
areas of government meet at
the Plaza of Three Powers,
which is a huge triangular
space.

Construction of Brasília
began in the late 1950s. Its
population is now approaching
one million.

▲ WHERE IS THE MOST
COLORFUL CARNIVAL
HELD?

**New Orleans and Nice are
among cities with famous
carnivals; but perhaps the
most colorful carnival takes
place in Rio de Janeiro, on
the southeast coast of Brazil.**

Rio de Janeiro's citizens hold
their carnival each year just
before Lent. Almost everyone
gets involved. Clubs and
societies prepare months
ahead. They hold contests to
find the best new songs and the
best fancy dress costumes.

At carnival time, gaily
colored flags and lights hang
from the buildings. Thousands
of singing, dancing citizens
take to the streets, together
with bands and displays borne
through the streets on wheeled
platforms. For a while, rich
and poor alike celebrate the
carnival.

Even outside carnival time
there is much to enjoy in this
great city. Gleaming white
beaches and tall mountain
peaks make Rio de Janeiro one
of the world's most spectacular
cities. Soaring above the city
are the high peaks of Sugar
Loaf Mountain (1,295 feet)
and Corcovado (2,310 feet). At
the summit of Corcovado is the
statue of Christ the Redeemer,
which is 98 feet high. Famous
beaches in Rio de Janeiro
include those of Ipanema and
Copacabana.

Rio de Janeiro is also a great
port and business center. But
there are shacks as well as fine
buildings. Thousands of
extremely poor people live in
slums on hills at the fringe of
the city center.

▼ WHICH COUNTRY IS THE WORLD'S LARGEST WOOL PRODUCER?

Australia produces more wool than any other country. More than a quarter of the world's wool comes from Australian sheep.

Australia produces so much wool because much of the country is suited for sheep raising. There are rich pastures and vast areas of grassland too dry for crops. Between them, both types of grassland can support 150 million or more sheep. This is more than ten sheep for every Australian person.

Australia's best-known wool producer is the merino. This is a hardy, heavy-fleeced breed of sheep suited to hot, dry climates. Thanks to the merino, Australia can produce more than 700,000 tons of wool in one year.

Other breeds are kept more for their meat. Australia is one of the world's top producers of mutton and lamb.

Drought sometimes destroys huge areas of grass. Then thousands of sheep may die of hunger and thirst.

▼ WHERE IS THE NULLARBOR PLAIN?

This great treeless plain got its name from the Latin words *nulla arbor*, meaning "no tree." The Nullarbor Plain lies in southern Australia close to the Great Australian Bight.

The Nullarbor Plain covers parts of the states of Western and South Australia. The plain is larger than Yugoslavia, and nearly as big as New Zealand.

The plain is low, flat and monotonous. Little rain falls.

▲ WHICH IS THE LARGEST AUSTRALIAN CITY?

The largest Australian city is Sydney, capital of the state of New South Wales. It has a population of over three million.

When it does rain, the water sinks down through holes in the rock, which is limestone, and forms underground lakes. There are no surface rivers, and the only plants to thrive are hardy shrubs such as saltbush.

There are only a few settlements along the Eyre highway and the trans-Australia railway, which both cross the Nullarbor Plain. The world's longest straight stretch of rail is 296 miles of track across the plain. The Nullarbor Plain is also the site of a rocket research center.

Sydney stands on the south-east coast of Australia, on one of the world's finest natural harbors. This is a series of deep-water inlets opening on the Pacific Ocean.

Sydney began in 1788 as a British prison settlement. It has grown into one of Australia's chief centers for business, manufacturing and the arts. The city makes ships, cars, textiles, chemical products and processed food. Its port exports farm products.

The city's famous buildings include Sydney Harbor Bridge, one of the world's largest steel-arch bridges. This links the main city center with suburbs on the northern shore of the harbor. Sydney Opera House, which was completed in 1973, overlooks the harbor. The white arches of its roof resemble the billowing sails of yachts.

▼ WHERE IS AYERS ROCK?

Ayers Rock is an immense stone outcrop near the center of Australia. It is famous as the largest rock on the earth's surface.

Ayers Rock stands in the Northern Territory, about 273 miles southwest of the town of Alice Springs. The rock is about 1½ miles long, 1 mile wide, and 5 miles around the base. It rises to a height of 1,100 feet from a low, sandy plain where only small, tough plants grow. The rock was left exposed after surrounding layers of rock were worn away by erosion.

From the air, the rock looks like a great stranded whale. At sunset, its bare sandstone slopes glow brilliant orange. Then they turn purple as the light starts to fade.

Long ago, Australian Aborigines made paintings on the walls of the caves in the rock. The first Europeans to see Ayers Rock arrived in 1872. Today, thousands of visitors to central Australia visit this huge outcrop.

▲ WHERE DID THE PEOPLE OF THE PACIFIC ISLANDS COME FROM?

Long ago, Stone Age peoples settled in thousands of islands far out in the Pacific Ocean. Groups reached the islands by canoe at different times from Asia.

There are three great groups of Pacific Islands, mostly in the South Pacific. The southwest group is Melanesia, or the "black islands." Their black-skinned islanders have frizzy hair and look like Negroes. Their ancestors may have come from Indonesia.

The northwest Pacific Islands are called Micronesia, or "little islands." The Micronesians are tall with light-brown skin. Micronesians probably spread east from Southeast Asia.

Most islands east of Melanesia and Micronesia belong to Polynesia, or "the many islands." Polynesians are tall and strongly built, with paler skins than the other islanders. Finds of old tools show that the early Polynesians most likely came from southern China.

▲ WHERE IS THE AUSTRALIAN OUTBACK?

The "outback" is a name for the remote, wild interior of Australia. Few people live in the outback. Most Australians live in towns and cities near the coast.

The Australian outback has a dry climate, and deserts cover much of the country. These bare lands include immense level plains where little but eucalyptus and acacia scrub grows. After the rains, desert areas are often covered with carpets of wild flowers.

In areas with more rainfall, there are vast sheep and cattle stations. In some rainier parts of the outback, near the coast, there are forests of giant eucalyptus trees.

Early explorers and settlers saw the outback as a place of adventure. But some died of hunger or thirst, lost in its deserts, or killed by its droughts. Even now, only skilled Aborigine hunters and food gatherers can survive without help in Australia's harsh, dry heartland.

109

▶ WHERE IS THE LONGEST BRIDGE?

The answer depends on how you measure bridge length. In the early 1980s the bridge with the greatest length between supports was the Humber Estuary Bridge in northeastern England.

The Humber Estuary Bridge crosses the River Humber's estuary near Hull in Humberside. This suspension bridge has a main span that measures 4,625 feet in length. The span is slung from cables supported by two giant towers. Each tower rises to a height of more than 531 feet. Because the earth's surface is curved, the towers are slightly farther apart at the top than at the bottom.

Including its two side spans, the Humber Estuary Bridge measures 7,283 feet in length. This is 1,060 feet shorter than the Mackinac Straits Bridge in Michigan.

Work on the Humber Bridge lasted from 1972 to 1980. Engineers first built foundations for the towers and anchorages at the ends of the bridge. Then they put up the towers. Next they hung the main cables and anchored them at each end of the bridge. Lastly they put the roadway in place.

▶ WHICH IS THE LARGEST COUNTRY?

The world's largest country is the USSR (Union of Soviet Socialist Republics), or Soviet Union for short. The USSR is more than twice the size of Canada, the second largest country.

REPUBLICS OF THE USSR

Russian SFSR (1)	Turkmenistan (5)	Tadzhikistan (9)	Lithuania (13)
Kazakhstan (2)	Armenia (6)	Ukraine (10)	Byelorussia (14)
Uzbekistan (3)	Georgia (7)	Estonia (11)	Moldavia (15)
Kirgizia (4)	Azerbaijan (8)	Latvia (12)	

The USSR covers an area of 8,649,500 square miles. It includes more than half of Europe and almost two-fifths of Asia. This makes the USSR larger than four of the world's seven continents.

The USSR stretches from the Baltic and Black seas in the west to the Pacific Ocean in the east. To the north is the Arctic Ocean and to the south are the countries of Turkey, Iran, Afghanistan, Mongolia and China.

Within the USSR there are many types of climate and countryside. In the north are vast areas of cold, treeless tundra and huge evergreen forests. Farther south are grasslands, mountains and deserts.

There are 15 republics in the USSR with their own cultures and languages. The largest is Russia, which stretches from Europe to Siberia. Russians make up more than half the population of the USSR. The capital city, Moscow, lies in Russia, and the official language of the USSR is Russian.

▲ WHERE IS THE TALLEST BUILDING?

▲ WHERE IS THE LONGEST ROAD TUNNEL?

▲ WHICH IS THE SMALLEST COUNTRY?

The world's tallest office building is the Sears Tower, in Chicago, Illinois. Its highest roof level rises 1,453 feet above the ground.

The Sears Tower stands on Wacker Drive in Chicago's central business district. Here land is so expensive that people build offices upward rather than outward.

The tower is an office block that looks like nine upended narrow glass boxes, some longer than others, joined at the sides. Steel frames inside support the walls, which are made of aluminum and dark glass. The building has 110 floors; 16,000 windows; 103 elevators; 18 escalators. More than 16,500 people work in it.

The Sears Tower is named after a mail-order firm which was originally called Sears, Roebuck and Company. The tower was built between 1970 and 1973. Some television masts and towers are even taller than the Sears Tower.

The world's longest road tunnel is the St. Gotthard Road Tunnel which runs beneath the Swiss Alps.

The St. Gotthard Road Tunnel is in southern Switzerland. It runs for 10 miles from Göschenen south to Airolo. The tunnel cuts through a huge mountain mass called the St. Gotthard Massif.

This mountain mass had always hindered travelers journeying through Switzerland on their way between Germany and Italy. After 1882 the St. Gotthard Rail Tunnel made travel easier, but the only road wound over a mountain pass made dangerous by deep snow in winter.

Cutting the St. Gotthard Road Tunnel began in 1970. Engineers worked toward each other from both ends. They met in 1976, and the two-lane tunnel opened in 1980.

The new road tunnel takes two hours off the road journey from north to south Switzerland. The tunnel is open all the year.

The world's smallest country is Vatican City, the Pope's official home. This country is an independent state within the country of Italy.

The Vatican stands in the city of Rome. It covers only 108 acres and is no bigger than many parks. Only about 700 people live in Vatican City.

The Vatican's main buildings are St. Peter's (the world's largest church) and the Vatican Palace, which has over a thousand rooms. There are chapels, apartments, offices, and a museum, library, and collection of documents.

Officials run the state's daily affairs. There is a governor, as well as a cardinal secretary of state, experts in law and money management, and legates (ambassadors) who go abroad.

The Vatican has its own police. The Swiss Guards, who wear uniforms of a style unchanged for centuries, act as the Pope's bodyguard. The Vatican issues its own stamps and newspapers.

▼ WHERE WERE THE SEVEN WONDERS OF THE WORLD?

These famous structures were built in lands near the eastern end of the Mediterranean Sea in ancient times. Antipater of Sidon drew up the list in the second century BC.

The Pyramids of Egypt were the tombs of Egyptian pharaohs. The Hanging Gardens of Babylon were terraced gardens in what is now Iraq. The Statue of Zeus at Olympia stood in Greece at the site of the first Olympic Games. It was 39 feet high and made of ivory, gold and gems. The Temple of Diana was a great marble temple built at Ephesus in what is now western Turkey. Also in Turkey was the Mausoleum of Halicarnassus, a tomb made for King Mausolus. The Colossus of Rhodes was a giant statue on the island of Rhodes. The Pharos of Alexandria was an Egyptian lighthouse which may have been 400 feet high. Of all these ancient structures, only the pyramids still exist.

▼ WHERE IS EASTER ISLAND?

Easter Island is a small, remote island in the South Pacific. It is famous for its mysterious giant stone heads and a strange writing system, both made by Stone Age peoples.

Easter Island lies 2,393 miles west of Chile and nearly half as far from Pitcairn, the nearest inhabited island.

Polynesians settled on Easter Island more than a thousand years ago. Their descendants built great stone burial platforms around the coast. On these they raised immense carved human heads, each weighing up to 50 tons. The Easter Islanders probably achieved this with just stone picks, ropes, ramps and pebble rollers. Easter Islanders also devised the *rongorongo* picture script, which no one can now decipher.

By 1872 wars, slave raids and disease had almost wiped out the islanders. But legends and finds of ancient tools have helped archaeologists piece together some of the island's past.

Pyramids of Egypt

Statue of Zeus at Olympia

Mausoleum of Halicarnassus

Temple of Diana

Pharos of Alexandria

Colossus of Rhodes

Hanging Gardens of Babylon

▼ WHERE IS THE HOME OF THE YETI?

The yeti is an ape-like beast which is supposed to live high up in the Himalaya Mountains of Asia.

The yeti is also known as the Abominable Snowman. Mountain people say that it lives on high snowy slopes, but will move down to attack villagers. They describe it as big, ape-like and hairy, with arms that hang to its knees. It supposedly walks upright on sturdy legs, like a human.

Tribespeople claim to have seen this creature, but no one has ever proved it exists. The British mountaineer Eric Shipton photographed "yeti" tracks which he found in snow near Mount Everest in 1951. But such big footprints could have been made by a bear. In 1954, the members of another expedition examined three "yeti" scalps which in fact had come from a rare goat-like mammal known as the serow.

Some people believe that the yeti may be a type of early human which has survived in the Himalayas to the present day.

▼ WHERE IS THE BERMUDA TRIANGLE?

The Bermuda Triangle is a popular name for a triangular patch of the Atlantic Ocean off the southeast United States. There are claims that many ships and planes have disappeared or met with unexplained accidents in the area of the triangle.

People disagree about the exact area of the triangle. Some suggest that its corners are formed by Florida and the islands of Bermuda and Puerto Rico.

More than 50 ships and 20 planes are said to have vanished inside the triangle. This is far more than you might expect for an area this size. In one disaster, five American bombers disappeared together in 1945. Tales also tell of crews missing from boats found with hot meals aboard.

Writers blame the disappearances on underwater volcanoes, strange forces or death rays from space. But storms, human error and mechanical faults could have caused the incidents.

▼ WHERE WAS ATLANTIS?

According to legend, Atlantis was a powerful island kingdom that used to lie in the Atlantic Ocean. Then, one day, it sank. Archaeologists think a real island gave rise to this legend.

The Greek philosopher Plato described Atlantis more than 2,300 years ago. Long before that, he declared, Atlantis had been a great island empire. Its armies overran many Mediterranean lands but were defeated by Athens. Later, earthquakes and floods struck Atlantis, and it sank swiftly under the sea.

Many people have believed that this story is true. Some thought that Atlantis was really America, the Canary Islands or the Bahamas.

In the 1960s, Greek archaeologists discovered that an ancient civilization had once flourished on a volcanic island known as Thera, or Santorini, in the Aegean Sea. In about 1450 BC the volcano exploded, destroying the civilization. It is possible that Thera was Atlantis.

113

TRANSPORTATION

▼ WHERE ARE THE
WORLD'S BUSIEST SEA
LANES?

**The busiest sea lanes are
narrow seas where many
ships carry cargo and
passengers to and from
industrial nations.**

The English Channel between
France and England is one of
the busiest sea lanes in the
world. The English Channel is
about 350 miles long and no
more than 21 miles wide at its
narrowest, between Dover and
Cap Gris-Nez. The Channel
joins the Atlantic Ocean to the
North Sea.

Each day, dozens of big
cargo ships sail through the
Channel to and from the great
ports of northern Europe. The
ships include oil tankers and
container vessels. Between
them they carry huge loads of
food, fuel, minerals and
manufactured goods.

▼ WHERE ARE THE MAIN OIL
SEA-ROUTES?

**Thousands of miles of sea
separate many oil-producing
countries from the chief oil-
consuming countries. The
main oil sea-routes cross the
oceans between them.**

Oil sea-routes run from oil-
producing countries such as
Saudi Arabia and Iran (on the
Persian Gulf), Indonesia,
Libya in North Africa, and
Venezuela in South America.
The routes lead to major oil
consumers such as the United
States, the nations of Western
Europe and Japan.

One of the main oil routes
leads from the Persian Gulf
down the coast of East Africa,
then around Africa's southern
tip and up the west coast to
North America and Western
Europe. Oil routes sailed by
supertankers end at deep-
water offshore terminals.

▼ WHERE IS THE WORLD'S
BUSIEST PORT?

**The busiest port is the
Rotterdam-Europoort in the
Netherlands. This handles
more cargo than any other
port in the world.**

The Rotterdam-Europoort lies
on the Nieuwe Maas, a branch
of the River Rhine. The New
Waterway canal links it with
the North Sea, 18 miles away.
The port covers about 38
square miles and is the largest
artificial harbor. Waterways
link the Rotterdam-Europoort
with other parts of the
Netherlands and with German
cities on the Rhine.

By the early 1980s this port
was handling from 253 to 286
million tons of seaborne cargo
every year. More than 29,000
seagoing ships and up to
200,000 barges were annually
using Rotterdam.

▼ WHERE DO ICEBREAKERS OPERATE?

Icebreakers are ships that operate where waterways freeze over thickly. They break the ice to let other ships through. At least one Russian icebreaker can crush ice 13 feet thick.

Icebreakers open passages through ice-covered lakes and seas. They work in the Great Lakes, the Baltic Sea and around the Arctic Ocean.

An icebreaker has a strong, heavy bow, armored sides and powerful engines. The bow is deeply undercut so that it can rear up on to the ice. The ship's crew pump water into forward tanks. This makes the bow heavy enough to crush the ice by sheer weight. The crew can also break the ice by shifting water inside the ship to make it rock from side to side.

Icebreakers have hulls especially strengthened and shaped to resist ice pressing in from the sides. The hulls must be broader than those of following ships, to leave them a wide enough passage.

▲ WHERE ARE LIGHTHOUSES BUILT?

Lighthouses are built mostly on or near coastal reefs and peninsulas, and at harbors and ports. Some lighthouses warn sailors of danger. Others help to guide them to a safe anchorage.

Lighthouses have been used for centuries to guide and warn sailors. The most famous ancient lighthouse was the Pharos of Alexandria, built in Egypt about 300 BC.

Early lighthouses were just wooden towers with metal baskets of burning wood or coal hung from poles on top. Many modern lighthouses are built of cast iron or reinforced concrete. Their lights are magnified by lenses so that they can be seen from great distances. The most powerful of all lights shines from the Creac'h d'Ouessant lighthouse. This warns of treacherous rocks off north-west France.

Most lighthouses have sirens that blare out coded fog-warnings. Some emit radio signals to guide ships with radio direction finders.

At anchor · Port side · Starboard side · Vessels approaching

▲ WHERE ARE THE NAVIGATION LIGHTS ON A SHIP?

This depends mostly on what the ship is doing and partly on the size of the ship.

The main navigation lights for a moving ship are the masthead light, sidelights and sternlight. Ships with hulls of 164 feet or more show two white masthead lights. The foremast light is 20 feet above the hull and is visible from ahead and either side. The mainmast light is higher than the foremast light and is visible for 6 miles.

There are two sidelights. The port light (left side) is red and the starboard light (right side) is green. Sidelights are lower than masthead lights and are also visible from ahead. The sternlight (at the back) is white.

Anchored vessels show one or more white lights, and light up their decks if they measure 328 feet or more. Ships that are towing show a yellow light at the stern.

▶ WHERE IS THE LONGEST RAILROAD?

The world's longest railroad is the Trans-Siberian Railroad that travels across the Soviet Union.

The Trans-Siberian Railroad was built to link European Russia with the Pacific Ocean in the Far East. The name means "across Siberia." Its track runs right across Siberia, the northern part of Asia. This Siberian stretch of track measures 4,592 miles from Chelyabinsk near the Ural Mountains to the port of Vladivostok on the Pacific Ocean.

You could take an even longer trip by joining the train at Moscow in European Russia. The distance from Moscow to Nakodhka, at the end of the line, is 5,852 miles.

This is the world's longest train journey. It involves 97 stops and lasts eight days.

In 1938, work started on making a short-cut to bypass a long southern loop around Lake Baikal. Laying this northern stretch of track involved shifting colossal quantities of earth and building 3,700 bridges. The new line was complete by 1983. It will shorten the journey across Siberia by 310 miles.

▶ WHERE DID THE ORIENT EXPRESS TRAVEL?

The Orient Express was a famous luxury passenger train that used to travel across Europe from west to east and back. Its name comes from *Orient*, another word for "east."

The Orient Express brought great style to rail travel in Europe. The train had a library, smoking-room, ladies' boudoir, dining car and sleeping cars.

People sat in red plush armchairs. They washed in bathrooms with mosaic floors and ate in a tapestry-lined dining car with an embossed leather ceiling.

The route of the train has changed several times since the name Orient Express was first used in 1883. At times wars and other problems have made

it impossible for trains to travel across all Europe.

At one time passengers could travel direct from Paris to the Turkish city of Istanbul, where Europe meets Asia. The train passed through Milan in Italy, Belgrade in Yugoslavia, and Sofia in Bulgaria. Today's nearest equivalent runs from Paris to Vienna in Austria and Bucharest in Romania.

In the early 1980s the Venice Simplon Orient Express began running between London and Venice. It brought back the luxury travel of the old-style Oriental Express.

▲ WHERE IS THE LONGEST ROAD?

The world's longest road is the Pan-American Highway. It runs from northwestern North American to the far south of South America.

The Pan-American Highway extends from Alaska to Chile. In fact it is not a single road, but a system of routes linking the countries of North and Central America and those of the west coast of South America.

The highway system remains incomplete. A stretch of swampy tropical forest, called the Darién Gap, separates Panama from Colombia and so cuts off the route between Central and South America.

American nations began planning a Pan-American road link in the 1920s. They had built most of the system by the early 1950s. South American countries paid for the parts of the highway within their own borders. The United States helped to pay for the section between Texas and Panama.

▲ WHERE DO PEOPLE USE RICKSHAWS?

People use rickshaws as taxis in East and Southeast Asia. They are light vehicles, often pulled or pedalled by a man, and usually carrying one passenger.

The name rickshaw comes from *jinrikisha*, which is made up of three Japanese words: *jin* (man), *riki* (power) and *sha* (vehicle).

Rickshaws were supposedly invented by a missionary to Japan in about 1870. A rickshaw has a chair-like body. It is covered with a movable hood and is mounted on springs. Early models had two large wheels with wire spokes, and two shafts. A passenger sat in the back and the rickshaw driver stood between the shafts, with which he pulled the rickshaw along. Pulling the rickshaw required great physical effort.

The use of rickshaws spread to China, India and Africa. Rickshaws with built-in cycles or motorcycle engines have mostly taken the place of the type that was pulled along.

▲ WHICH CITY HAD THE FIRST UNDERGROUND RAILWAY?

London was the world's first city to have an underground railway. The first part of this system was opened in 1863.

London needed an underground railway system by the 1860s. The city was growing fast and its streets were becoming crowded with slow, horse-drawn traffic.

Because London stands on soft clay, it was fairly easy to drive tunnels under the city. The workers dug down from street level to make the first shallow, underground track. This was built for steam trains.

Later, engineers cut new tunnels at deeper levels for railway lines served by electric passenger trains. The London underground now has a number of interlinked lines that cover 254 miles.

Today, many cities have underground railways. They include Paris, Milan, New York and Moscow.

Different types of planes travel at a variety of altitudes, or heights. How high a plane flies depends largely on what it was designed for, and on regulations laid down by authorities that control air traffic.

Small, propeller-driven planes fly mostly at fairly low levels – high enough to avoid dangers such as mountains and tall structures, but below the flight paths that are used by jet airliners.

Jet airliners often fly at a height of about 30,000 feet. *Concorde*, a supersonic airliner, flies even higher. Flying high helps planes to keep above rough weather. But air-traffic controllers assign flight levels to planes to prevent them colliding.

Some military planes can reach amazing altitudes. The American Lockheed SR-71 spy plane can fly 19 miles high, and a Russian "Foxbat" (MiG-25) has soared to an incredible height of 23 miles.

MiG-25 'Foxbat'

In 1981 an airport at Jeddah in western Saudi Arabia became the world's largest. Two years later, Saudi Arabia completed an even larger airport, shown here in the picture, at the capital, Riyadh.

King Abdul-Aziz International Airport at Jeddah was built mainly to receive the nearly two million Muslim pilgrims who visit Mecca each year.

The airport site covers 45 square miles. There are two main runways and four terminals. The Haj terminal, the world's largest roofed building, covers more than half a square mile. In style it resembles a cluster of nomads' tents, but it has marble walls and glass-fiber roofs.

In 1983, the even larger King Khaled Airport opened at Riyadh. This also has two runways and four terminals. There is a royal pavilion, as well as covered parking for 7,700 cars, and buildings for the people who live and work there.

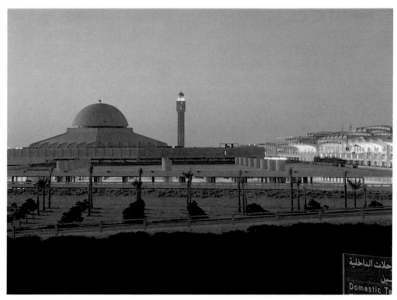

جلالت الداخلية

Domestic Te

The busiest air routes are those between certain cities in North America, and over parts of Europe.

A good indication of where the most air traffic occurs is the number of people passing through different airports. Chicago International Airport handles the most flights. Nearly a quarter of a million people arrived at or left the airport in 1980. Over 43 million people passed through it. Most were taking flights to or from other American cities.

The next busiest airport is Hartsfield International Airport at Atlanta, Georgia. A new terminal, opened in 1980, allows it to cope with up to 60 million people a year.

The busiest international airport is Heathrow Airport, London. By the early 1980s Heathrow handled more than 28 million passengers a year.

On average, more than two and a half times as many people fly in North America as in the next busiest areas: Europe and Russia.

▼ WHERE DID THE WORST AIR ACCIDENT HAPPEN?

The worst accident in the history of air travel happened at Tenerife, one of the Canary Islands off north-west Africa. More than 500 people died when two jumbo jets collided there before take-off in 1977.

The disaster took place at Los Rodeos Airport on 27 March, 1977. The airport was crowded with planes which had been diverted there after a terrorists' bomb had exploded at a big airport on a nearby island.

A Dutch KLM Boeing 747 and a Pan-Am Boeing 747 were taxiing for take-off in mist and drizzle. The Dutch plane struck the Pan-Am plane and both burst into flames. All the 248 people aboard the Dutch plane died, and 335 perished on the other aircraft. There were over 60 survivors.

Pilot error, poor visibility and lack of radar at the airport helped to cause this terrible disaster. Nobody had noticed when one plane moved into the other's path.

▲ WHERE AND WHAT IS A "BLACK BOX"?

The "black box" is the popular name for a flight recorder, a device carried in aircraft. Its purpose is to reveal the cause of faults if these develop in flight.

Flight recorders show how aircraft systems behave. They give information about a plane's heading, height, air speed, rate of descent and so on. On some recorders, the information appears as lines engraved on a strip of metal foil. This is housed in a crashproof, fireproof, floatable box. In a crash the box is hurled clear and recovered later. There are also digital recorders which record the information in binary code.

Besides a flight recorder, airliners carry a cockpit voice recorder to record aircrew conversations. Between them, the flight recorder and voice recorder help experts to learn what caused a crash, even if all aboard were killed. Such information helps designers to produce safer planes.

▼ WHERE CAN ENGINES BE POSITIONED IN AN AIRCRAFT?

Engineers can position aircraft engines anywhere where they will work without unbalancing the plane in flight.

All aircraft engines must be placed where pipes can feed fuel to them from storage tanks. Piston engines, turbojets and turbo-props must all be able to suck in air from the front and force out air or hot gases from the back, to thrust a plane forward.

Piston engines and turbo-prop engines spin airscrews (propellers) that push or pull a plane along. "Puller" airscrews project forward from engines mounted in the nose or wings. A few planes have pusher airscrews jutting backward from wing-mounted engines. There are even push-pull twin-engined aircraft, with airscrews at both ends.

Airliners have turbo-jets built into or slung below the wings, or on the rear fuselage. Fast warplanes have turbo-jets in or alongside the fuselage.

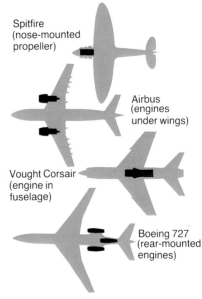

Spitfire (nose-mounted propeller)

Airbus (engines under wings)

Vought Corsair (engine in fuselage)

Boeing 727 (rear-mounted engines)

INDEX

Page numbers in *italics* refer to pictures

PHOTOGRAPHIC ACKNOWLEDGMENTS

14 top D. Bridgewater, bottom Geoscience Features; 15 top De Beers, bottom J. Allan Cash Photo Library; 16 top ZEFA, bottom Hawaiian Travel Center; 17 top Solarfilma, Iceland, bottom BBC Hulton Picture Library; 18 bottom ZEFA; 20 left ZEFA, middle Geoslides, right David and Jill Wright; 21 top ZEFA, bottom Tony Morrison; 22 bottom Geoslides; 25 bottom Israel Tourist Office; 26 top Xinhua News Agency, bottom Paul Popper; 27 top J. Allan Cash Photo Library, bottom ZEFA; 28 bottom ZEFA; 29 bottom ZEFA, top Xinhua News Agency/ZEFA; 30 Photri/ZEFA; 31 top ZEFA, bottom Allan Hutchison; 32 top Royal Netherlands Embassy; 33 left David and Jill Wright, middle Lanecott Co, right J. Allan Cash Photo Library; 36 top ZEFA, bottom ZEFA; 37 top left Institute of Geological Sciences, London, bottom Geoscience Features, top right David and Jill Wright; 64 bottom left Associated press; 73 middle British Library; 77 top BBC Hulton Picture Library, bottom Paul Popper; 80 top J. Nance/J. Hillelson; 84 top ZEFA, middle ZEFA, bottom Italian Ministry of Defense; 85 top ZEFA, middle Geoscience Features, bottom ZEFA; 86 top ZEFA, bottom Jane Taylor/Sonia Halliday; 87 top Dave Collins, bottom left F. H. C. Birch/Sonia Halliday, bottom right ZEFA; 88 bottom J. Allan Cash Photo Library; 89 top ZEFA, bottom left Sonia Halliday; 90 top Italian State Tourist Office, middle ZEFA, bottom ZEFA; 91 top ZEFA, bottom Sonia Halliday; 92 top Sonia Halliday, middle Jane Taylor/Sonia Halliday, bottom ZEFA; 93 top Geoscience Features, middle ZEFA, bottom J. Allan Cash Photo Library; 94 top Dave Collins, middle J. Allan Cash Photo Library; 95 top ZEFA, middle Singapore Tourist Office; 96 bottom Japan Tourist Office; 97 top ZEFA, 98 top left ZEFA, bottom James Wellard/Sonia Halliday; 99 top J. Allan Cash Photo Library, bottom ZEFA; 100 top ZEFA; 101 top C. R. Warn, middle ZEFA; 102 middle B. J. Cruickshank, bottom Geoscience Features; 103 top Space Frontiers, middle Geoscience Features, bottom J. Allan Cash Photo Library; 104 top ZEFA, middle J. Allan Cash Photo Library, bottom British Museum; 105 right ZEFA, left J. Allan Cash Photo Library; 106 top Robert Harding, bottom ZEFA; 107 top ZEFA, bottom ZEFA; 108 Australian News and Information Bureau; 110 top ZEFA; 111 left J. Allan Cash Photo Library, middle ZEFA, right Jane Taylor/Sonia Halliday; 112 bottom right ZEFA; 113 right J. Allan Cash Photo Library; 118 top Saudi Airlines; 119 top Central Press Photos.

Picture research: Jackie Cookson